The Political Writings of Dr Johnson

Dr. Samuel Johnson, who showed a lifelong interest in politics and political history, produced more writings in this field than is usually recognized. Until now, these have existed for the modern reader only in complete editions of his works. The aim of the present edition is to make the most important of them more readily accessible.

Spanning the years from 1756 to 1775, it includes Johnson's comments on the Seven Years' War, the controversy that surrounded Wilkes after the Middlesex elections, Britain's strained relations with Spain over the Falkland Islands, the electioneering of 1774, and the Americans' struggle for Independence.

Such a contemporary viewpoint of important issues and events is obviously of prime importance to the historian of the period. In writing his pamphlets of the 1770's Johnson consistently supported the government; indeed, his pamphlet on the Falkland Islands clearly draws, as Boswell informs us, 'upon materials furnished to him by the ministry'. Yet, notwithstanding his partisan approach, Johnson writes throughout with a characteristic conviction and assurance. Even Boswell, who was by no means always in sympathy with the political viewpoint expressed, rightly paid tribute to the quality of the writing in these pamphlets.

This material contains some of Johnson's best prose, and for this reason alone merits the attention of every student of English literature.

Professor Hardy has made a selection of the most important political pieces, related to Johnson's own life and to the political and historical movements of the eighteenth century. An Introduction and extensive Notes are provided, enabling the student reader to approach these writings with an informed awareness of the political and historical issues involved.

The selection will be of great value to students of the eighteenth century, particularly to those who are concerned with the interaction of literary, political and historical affairs.

The Political Writings of Dr Johnson

The Political Writings of Dr Johnson

a selection

edited by
J. P. Hardy
Professor of English, University of New England

NEW YORK
BARNES & NOBLE, INC.

*First published in the United States of America 1968
by Barnes & Noble, Inc., New York, N.Y.*
© *J. P. Hardy 1968*

Printed in Great Britain

To my Mother and Father

Contents

Introduction   page ix
i. Johnson's Early Political Works   ix
ii. The *Literary Magazine* and *Universal Chronicle*   xi
iii. Pamphlets   xiv
iv. Text   xxi

Text

1 *An Introduction to the Political State of Great-Britain*   1
2 *Observations on His Britannic Majesty's Treaties with Her Imperial Majesty of All the Russia's and the Landgrave of Hesse-Cassel*   18
3 *Observations on the Present State of Affairs*   23
4 *Observations* (August–September 1758)   32
5 *The False Alarm*   39
6 *Thoughts on the Late Transactions respecting Falkland's Islands*   60
7 *The Patriot*   91
8 *Taxation No Tyranny*   100

Notes   133

Index   149

vii

Introduction

Dr. Samuel Johnson, the outstanding literary figure of his age, showed a lifelong interest in politics and political history. He wrote far more of a political nature than is usually realised, without ever being (what he so much deplored) 'a scribbler for a party'. Though he received a pension of £300 per annum in 1762, his later conservative tracts in support of the government are, no less than his youthful pieces, written with conviction. In every instance they may be taken to express what he felt at the time to be the truth of the question. His concern for this is, as early as his thirtieth year, characteristically reflected in a letter to the *Gentleman's Magazine*. 'Political truth', he writes, 'is undoubtedly of very great importance, and they who honestly endeavour after it are doubtless engaged in a laudable pursuit.'

Johnson's Early Political Works

During his early years in the capital Johnson was the author of several works attacking Walpole's administration. Even his first great poem *London* (May 1738), an imitation in the Augustan manner of Juvenal's third satire on Rome, contained overt anti-Walpole allusions, and was, perhaps, primarily a political satire.[1] In his *Marmor Norfolciense* of the following April Johnson, writing under the name of 'Probus Britannicus', fictitiously recounts the discovery, in Walpole's home county and constituency, of a stone bearing an inscription in Latin verse which openly alluded to those evils with which the opposition was charging the court and administration—standing armies, the dangerous ascendancy of France, and the subordination of British to Hanoverian interests. Assuming the role of pedantic commentator, Johnson indulges his wit at the expense of the government in pretending to stumble

---

[1] *v.* my forthcoming article, 'Johnson's *London:* The Country vs. the City', in *Studies in the Eighteenth Century*, ed R. F. Brissenden.

Introduction

over lines of which the import is plain and unequivocal. More pedestrian as a sustained piece of irony is his *Compleat Vindication of the Licensers of the Stage* which, published the following month, attacked the Stage Licensing Act of 1737 on the occasion of the Lord Chamberlain's refusal to grant a licence to Henry Brooke's *Gustavus Vasa*. This play has been aptly described by Professor D. J. Greene, in the only full-length study of Johnson's political writings, as 'a barefaced allegory of the state of England as portrayed in opposition propaganda'.[1]

Another anti-Walpole tract by Johnson was also published at this time. Appearing in the *Gentleman's Magazine* for June 1738, it served to introduce a famous series of debates—under the guise of 'Debates in the Senate of Magna Lilliputia'—designed to inform readers of the proceedings of parliament. At first Johnson seems to have been employed by the editor Edward Cave in revising those written by William Guthrie. Later he was (according to Boswell) 'sole composer'—probably for those debates occurring between 25 November 1740 and 25 February 1743, and published in the *Gentleman's Magazine* between July 1741 and March 1744.[2] Boswell's word 'composer' is well chosen. Johnson apparently worked from brief notes supplied to him by others, Professor B. B. Hoover, the best-informed student of his *Debates*, concluding that he may be described as 'not simply the reporter but the author'.[3] That Johnson wrote the speeches was not generally known. Moreover, though he once claimed to have taken care that 'the WHIG DOGS should not have the best of it', he does not appear to have been obviously partisan. Perhaps in this schooling-ground for the political writer he came to moderate his enthusiasm for opposition and be more critical of 'patriots' and the rancour of parties.

During the next decade virtually no demands were made on Johnson's political pen. It was not until 1756, a year which saw both the advent of the *Literary Magazine* and the beginning of the Seven Years' War, that Johnson was again to participate actively in political writing. Of particular interest in the meantime, how-

[1] *The Politics of Samuel Johnson* (1960), p. 99.
[2] *Boswell's Life of Johnson*, ed. G. B. Hill, rev. L. F. Powell (1934–50), I. 502; B. B. Hoover, *Samuel Johnson's Parliamentary Reporting* (1953), p. 19 and Appendix II.
[3] Hoover, p. 129.

Introduction

ever, is a paragraph from his preface to Dodsley's *Preceptor* (1748):

> The principles of *laws* and *government* come next to be consider'd; by which men are taught to whom obedience is due, for what it is paid, and in what degree it may be justly required. This knowledge by peculiar necessity constitutes a part of the education of an *Englishman*, who professes to obey his prince according to the law, and who is himself a secondary *legislator*, as he gives his consent by his representative, to all the laws by which he is bound, and has a right to petition the great council of the nation, whenever he thinks they are deliberating upon an act detrimental to the interest of the community. (I. xxix)

Here Johnson outlines the subject's rights and duties within the peculiarly British system of constitutional monarchy. Another interesting item written during this decade is the Preface to the first Index of the *Gentleman's Magazine* (1753), which was attributed to Johnson by Dr. L. F. Powell in 1943.[1] It contains an unqualified complimentary reference to Walpole and a dismissal of the Forty-Five as a 'contemptible' rebellion.

The Literary Magazine and Universal Chronicle

The first three pieces in this present volume have been taken from the *Literary Magazine*. The primary aim of this periodical, which ran into a third year, was to give (as Johnson stated in its preface) 'the history political and literary of every month'. His own contributions, numerous throughout the first year, were political rather than literary. In his *Introduction to the Political State of Great-Britain*, which opened the first issue for May, he sets out to review present events in the light of British colonial and foreign policy from the reign of Elizabeth to that of George II. Throughout he shows himself sensitive to national interests within the larger European scene, not only charging James I with culpable weakness in refusing to stand up to emerging foreign powers, especially France, but stigmatising also Walpole's later policy of appeasement. Johnson condemns all who act solely from motives of greed and personal interest, characteristically reminding his audience that 'no people can be great who have ceased to be virtuous'. His feelings of humanity were especially outraged at

[1] *Essays and Studies*, XXVIII (1943), 38–41.

Introduction

British exploitation of the North American natives. The French, on the other hand, had gained their allegiance by treating them better, and were for this reason seen as a distinct threat to the commercial interests and expansion of the British colonies.

With the outbreak of the Franco-British conflict in America, the possibility of an attack on Hanover, and perhaps even England itself, had also to be faced. Though a series of diplomatic moves led to a re-alignment of the European powers, Britain had meantime negotiated subsidy treaties with Russia and Hesse-Cassel. A substantial increase in the standing army was too unpopular a measure for the government to carry through. The Militia Bill, which in Johnson's view had much to recommend it, was also ultimately defeated in the House of Lords. Another course for increasing the military strength of the nation was to hire foreign troops in its service. In the *Literary Magazine* Johnson published abstracts of the Anglo-Hessian and Russian treaties of 1755, together with his own *Observations* upon them. Though he extensively reports the arguments on both sides, his sympathies are clearly with the 'advocates for the independence of Britain'. Even those who support the treaties merely to allay the fear of a French invasion are said to consider the introduction of mercenaries as 'the desperate remedy of desperate distress'. At times Johnson's phrases have an unmistakably Churchillian ring:

> Nature has stationed us in an island inaccessible but by sea, and we are now at war with an enemy...
>
> That we are able to defend our own country, that arms are most safely intrusted to our own hands, and that we have strength, and skill, and courage...
>
> ...and therefore it will not be easy to persuade the nation, a nation long renowned for valour, that it can need the help of foreigners to defend it from invasion.
>
> Those men are most likely to fight bravely... who fight for their own houses and farms, for their own wives and children.

In his *Observations on the Present State of Affairs*, published in the *Literary Magazine* for August, Johnson reviews the events in America which led up to the declaration of war between France and Britain. He begins by censuring both parties for their unjust and indefensible usurpation of another's territory. The happiness of people, the welfare of society, was to him of supreme importance;

Introduction

and so liberal are his sentiments on behalf of 'the natural lords and original inhabitants' that he concludes: 'Such is the contest that no honest man can heartily wish success to either party.' At the same time he realised that other, more pressing considerations now entered the reckoning, that the American situation had to be analysed in terms of present events. Between two powerful, rival nations conflict had become inevitable, especially since the French, originally confined to the less attractive parts of the continent, had more to gain by hostility than the British. Having begun to infiltrate southwards, they posed an immediate threat to the British colonies. Past successes had given them confidence. They also had the support of the Indians. And so Johnson realistically acknowledges their advantages, and is prepared to see the importance of the American theatre of war in Britain's more general struggle with France.

The next series of *Observations* included in this volume appeared in the *Universal Chronicle* for 1758, the weekly paper which was currently publishing Johnson's *Idler*. First attributed to him in 1942 by Professor Boylston Green,[1] these provide comments on news from various theatres of war, as well as on its reception in England. Johnson asks his readers to exercise sanity and restraint, whatever reports of defeat or victory may reach them. In his column for 26 August he celebrates the capture of the French fortress Louisburg, at the same time trying to assess impartially the significance of this gain. In a later column, which may be compared with *Idler* 20, Johnson warns the nation not to lose its sense of perspective by becoming delirious with joy over an enemy loss far from the French mainland. This drew from one correspondent a rebuke which was then tartly returned. Johnson's sarcasm seems to have been warranted, for his assailant had in his enthusiasm gone so far as to imply that the capture even of Paris itself would have been a victory of less importance.

Several other pieces of political interest were published about this time. The first volume of the *Literary Magazine* also contained Johnson's comments on the Militia Bill, *Observations* on a letter from 'Gallo-Anglus', 'a French refugee in America', *Memoirs of the King of Prussia*, a number of vigorous passages in defence of Admiral Byng (executed for his conduct off Minorca),

[1] *Yale University Library Gazette*, XVI (1942), 70–9.

Introduction

and reviews of Thomas Blackwell's *Memoirs of the Court of Augustus* and of Lewis Evans' *Essays on the Middle British Colonies in America*. Together with two items published during the last year of George II's reign—Johnson's preface to *Proceedings of the Committee for cloathing French Prisoners of War*, and a sympathetic review of William Tytler's defence of Mary Queen of Scots against the accepted interpretation of the 'casket' letters—these pieces help to show the range of his interest in political and historical matters.

During the first half of the next decade Johnson was busy with his edition of Shakespeare's plays. Afterwards he was engaged in helping friends—writing election addresses for Henry Thrale,[1] and contributing to the lectures of Robert Chambers, Vinerian Professor of Law at Oxford. Professor E. L. McAdam has collected the Johnsonian portions which, though they lie beyond the scope of this volume, merit the attention of every student of Johnson's politics.[2]

Pamphlets

The political writings for which Johnson is best remembered all appeared in the 1770s during the administrations of the Duke of Grafton and Lord North: *The False Alarm, Thoughts on the Late Transactions respecting Falkland's Islands, The Patriot,* and *Taxation No Tyranny*. Because of these pamphlets, especially the first and last, Johnson is today often regarded as a Tory diehard. Yet in each he was stating what at the time seemed to many the reasonable view.

The following events led to the publication of *The False Alarm* in January 1770. After the Middlesex election of the previous April, when the colourful demagogue John Wilkes had won yet another victory at the polls by overwhelmingly defeating his nearest rival Colonel Henry Lawes Luttrell, the House of Commons, having expelled for a second time the already imprisoned Wilkes, voted his opponent duly elected on the grounds that

---

[1] J. D. Fleeman, 'Dr. Johnson and Henry Thrale, M.P.', *Johnson, Boswell and their Circle* (essays presented to L. F. Powell), ed. M. M. Lascelles, J. L. Clifford, J. D. Fleeman, J. P. Hardy (1965), pp. 170-89.
[2] *Dr. Johnson and the English Law* (1951), pp. 81-120.

Introduction

Wilkes himself had been ineligible as a candidate. Meantime petitions on Wilkes' behalf began to circulate throughout the length and breadth of England; while in December Junius penned a notorious letter to the King in which he referred to 'the continued violation of the laws and . . . last enormous attack on the vital principles of the constitution', and then went on to deplore the transfer of the right of election '. . . from the collective to the representative body'.[1] Johnson, however, defended the House's action as constitutional, arguing that it had a legal right, and one clearly defensible on moral grounds in the present instance, to exercise the power of jurisdiction over its members. By a vote of the House Wilkes had been declared 'incapable of being elected a member to serve in this present parliament', and Johnson therefore held that his expulsion entailed present exclusion. Those, on the other hand, who supported Wilkes, maintained that he could not be excluded by a mere resolution of the House, Sir William Meredith, himself an M.P., citing Sir Edward Coke's judgment that 'he which is eligible of common Right, cannot be disabled, unless it be by Act of Parliament'.[2] No cast-iron precedent, it was felt, supported the House's action in excluding Wilkes once the majority of electors had decided in his favour.

That parliament should so trespass on the rights of the electorate today strikes us as wrong. History has accordingly condemned Johnson's pamphlet as reactionary and illiberal, one recent author having dismissed it as 'specious and discreditable', the work of a servile pensioner.[3] A sense of historical perspective should, however, allow us to pass a more balanced judgment. When Johnson's pamphlet was written, the independence of the House of Commons was regarded as one of the corner-stones of liberty. In defending its action in excluding Wilkes, Johnson was, in fact, upholding its autonomy. Nor did the character of the offending party persuade him to think differently, despite the popular outcry that liberty was being threatened. The whole tenor of his pamphlet is that the 'alarm' expressed by the opposition was 'false'. Not only was

---

[1] *The Letters of Junius*, ed. C. W. Everett (1927), p. 140.
[2] *Letter to Dr. Blackstone by the Author of The Question Stated* (1770), p. 48.
[3] Peter Quennell, *Four Portraits: Studies of the Eighteenth Century* (1945), p. 230.

Introduction

Wilkes a brazen opportunist rather than a sincere and lifelong reformer, but his cause was supported by the least responsible elements in the state. These Johnson viewed with profound suspicion, being convinced of the danger of allowing the uneducated classes a voice in the affairs of parliament. One of his most brilliantly written passages, meriting inclusion in any select anthology of English prose, describes 'the progress of a petition' and warns against an appeal to the 'rabble'. Later he emphatically made the same point in *The Patriot*:

> He is no lover of his country, that unnecessarily disturbs its peace. Few errors, and few faults of government can justify an appeal to the rabble; who ought not to judge of what they cannot understand, and whose opinions are not propagated by reason, but caught by contagion.

This was not an argument contrived merely on behalf of the government. Johnson's desire for order was genuine and deep-seated, and an ordered government in his view implied on the one hand a lawful authority and the right to govern, and on the other a willingness to obey and be governed. The Commons had to possess more than a 'nominal authority, to which perhaps obedience never may be paid'. For him a more important principle was at stake than that 'the right of electors must not be violated'. To state this clearly was Johnson's aim, who seems genuinely to have intended his pamphlet as a contribution to 'the science of government'.

From this it will be clear that Johnson was neither radical nor egalitarian. He was not a political ancestor of those who agitated for the Reform Bill of 1832. Nor did he ever put himself forward as the advocate of a classless society. Boswell reports that Mrs. Macaulay wondered how Johnson 'could reconcile his political principles with his moral; his notions of inequality and subordination with wishing well to the happiness of all mankind'. To this he had a ready answer: 'Why, Sir, I reconcile my principles very well, because mankind are happier in a state of inequality and subordination'. On another occasion he said: 'Sir, I am a friend to subordination, as most conducive to the happiness of society.' With this as his settled conviction, he had no qualms about opposing what seemed to him mere rabble-rousing. At the same

Introduction

time he would not have thought that such a view called his humanity into question.

This humanity is clearly evident in his next pamphlet. Published in March 1771, *Thoughts on the Late Transactions respecting Falkland's Islands* examines the conflicting claims of England and Spain to that remote territory. Events there had led to a diplomatic crisis between the two nations in 1770-1. Drawing on original documents for much of his material, Johnson gives a lucid account of this episode of British history. In brief, the Spanish had forcibly evicted a small garrison established on Saunders Island. In January 1771, after lengthy negotiations, Spain promised satisfaction for the injury and the restoration of Port Egmont, without at the same time agreeing to abandon the question of prior sovereignty. By the Spanish declaration England gained, as Johnson points out, all that had been asked. Taking the enlightened view that it would be foolish to risk reprisals by further demands, he engages in a vehement and impassioned denunciation of the warmongering of the opposition. As he questions its motives for seeking to precipitate a conflict, he paints a vivid and compelling picture of the harsh realities of war.

In fact, this pamphlet is distinguished for more than its clear exposition of issues and events and sanity of outlook. It is also one of Johnson's most impressive prose pieces. In few other places is his rhetoric so expressive or varied. Here especially he achieves an amplitude as well as a memorable incisiveness of style. Besides the original sarcasm on Grenville (*v*. p. 143), there are the contemptuous references to Chatham, Bellas and Beckford; while the elaborate description of Junius is an unrivalled *tour de force*.

Johnson's next pamphlet *The Patriot*, published in November 1774, was an attempt to lay down guidelines for voters at the forthcoming election. The previous parliament had been dissolved early to allow a new one to be returned before events in America reached a fresh crisis. On the day of its dissolution (30 September), a correspondent wrote to the *Middlesex Journal* complaining that 'patriotism, that god of electioneering idolatry, hath been the pretence of many of our parliamentary candidates'. In similar vein the anonymous author of *Vox Populi*, election propaganda which appeared in the same month as *The Patriot*, warned electors

Introduction

to 'beware of those who, in a former parliament, have turned out FALSE patriots'. In his revised Dictionary of 1773, Johnson contemptuously describes the self-styled 'patriot' as 'a factious disturber of government'. In his pamphlet on this topic, however, he cleverly takes the opportunity of contrasting the virtue of genuine patriotism with the misguided clamour and counterfeit zeal of the professed 'patriots'. These men were in no sense lovers of their country, and the electorate was expected to recognise as much, and to vote instead for the true patriot.

Throughout his pamphlet Johnson subjects to close scrutiny the commonplaces of the opposition. The popular agitation for parliamentary reform is dismissed as entirely and maliciously self-interested rather than genuinely and constructively disinterested; while in dealing with the opposition's criticism of foreign affairs Johnson both reiterates what he had said in his previous pamphlet and anticipates the central argument of *Taxation No Tyranny*. Censure is passed on those who not only seek irresponsibly to involve Britain in a war with Spain, but also disregard, on grounds of mere expediency, those obligations which the American colonies were thought to owe to the mother country.

Johnson's last great pamphlet was published in March 1775, when a final rupture with the colonies was imminent. During the previous decade Anglo-American relations had been exacerbated by the Stamp Act of 1765 (the first attempt to raise money in the colonies through direct taxes levied by the British parliament), Townshend's Revenue Act of 1767, the presence of English troops in America and the 'Boston Massacre' of 1770, the continuing impost on tea (resulting, in December 1773, in the dumping of a consignment of East India tea in Boston harbour), the British retaliatory, coercive legislation of the following spring—the Boston Port Act (closing the port), the Massachusetts Bay Regulating Act, the Impartial Administration of Justice Act, the Quartering Act (providing for the billeting of troops on private property)—the Quebec Act of the same year (interpreted by the Americans as a further punitive measure) and the contemptuous reception Britain gave to the proceedings of the Continental Congress which began at Philadelphia on 5 September. To the resolutions of this body *Taxation No Tyranny* was explicitly an answer.

The argument which Johnson opposed found expression not

Introduction

only in the colonists' cry of 'no taxation without representation', but also in a quotation, from the French historian Phillipe de Comines, which appeared on the title-page of Matthew Robinson-Morris's *Considerations on the Measures carrying on with respect to the British Colonies in North-America* (1774). According to Comines,

> There is neither King or Sovereign Lord on earth who has beyond his own domain power to lay one farthing on his subjects without the grant and consent of those who pay it, unless he does it by tyranny and violence.

The very title of Johnson's pamphlet, however, expresses a different view. He maintains that 'the supreme power of every community has the right of requiring from all its subjects such contributions as are necessary to the public safety or public prosperity'. As subjects of the British Crown, the colonists were bound to pay any tax laid upon them by the home government. True, they were not personally represented; but in this respect they were no different from many other subjects living within the realm. By their voluntary emigration to America they had voluntarily forfeited any rights of representation they might otherwise have had. And since Britain assumed responsibility for their defence, it was, in Johnson's view, only fair that they should make a contribution to the expense involved.

In taking this stand Johnson was, of course, opposing the tide of history. A new nation had already been born: 'for generations the inhabitants of these maturing colonies had been moving in the direction of home rule.'[1] As Professor Bernard Bailyn has stated, 'What was essentially involved in the American Revolution was ... the realization, the comprehension and fulfillment, of what was taken to be America's destiny in the context of world history.'[2] Extending back into the preceding century, and affecting the consciousness of a large segment of the American population, was a profound suspicion of English institutions and authority. Yet Johnson's short-sightedness can easily be exaggerated. Many responsible Englishmen held similar views; while even Americans were divided on the question. Only ten years previously James

---

[1] J. R. Alden, *The American Revolution 1775–1783* (1954), p. 4.
[2] *Pamphlets of the American Revolution 1750–1776* (1965–), I. 17.

Introduction

Otis had written in his pro-American *Vindication of the British Colonies:*

> The supreme legislative indeed represents the whole society or community, as well the dominions as the realm; and this is the true reason why the dominions are justly bound by such acts of Parliament as name them. This is implied in the idea of a supreme sovereign power; and if the Parliament had not such authority the colonies would be independent, which none but rebels, fools, or madmen will contend for. God forbid these colonies should ever prove undutiful to their mother country! Whenever such a day shall come it will be the beginning of a terrible scene.[1]

Otis was here thinking of the anarchy and bloodshed that would follow in America itself, whereas Johnson's was an Anglo-centric view prompted by his deep conviction that the colonies should willingly submit to both the authority and national interest of Britain. Like George III himself, he advocated American submission rather than British conciliation.

Not all Englishmen viewed the matter so inflexibly. A parliamentary minority, including Chatham, had consistently opposed the ministry; and the Rockinghams, though admitting British supremacy over the colonies, had always pointed out the inadvisability of insisting upon it. Moreover, to judge from the numerous replies to Johnson's pamphlet, many other Englishmen must have sympathised with the Americans. *Taxation, Tyranny*, published the same year, cleverly attempted to refute Johnson out of his own mouth. Since he admits that every charter 'is liable by its nature to change or revocation', his anonymous critic rightly points out that he should, to be consistent, have enumerated 'those circumstances which can justify a change or revocation' (pp. 18–19). The truth is that, with respect to the colonies, Johnson interpreted differently what he called in an earlier pamphlet 'the great and pregnant principle of political necessity'. Accepting the maxim that 'every act of government aims at publick good', he could not believe that the repeal of provincial charters would be in any way beneficial. 'By such repeal', he writes, 'the whole fabrick of subordination is immediately destroyed, and the constitution sunk at once into a chaos; the society is dissolved

[1] *Pamphlets of the American Revolution*, I. 565.

Introduction

into a tumult of individuals, without authority to command, or obligation to obey.'

Yet at this point, quite apart from the general constitutional question, one cannot fail to notice how much Johnson was a stickler for obedience. While he could readily drink to the next insurrection of slaves in the West Indies, he was nevertheless a lover of discipline almost for its own sake. Throughout *Taxation No Tyranny* one constantly feels that the argument was congenial to him, that he was inclined by temperament to favour coercive measures, that he thought the American colonists should be made to kiss the rod. Indeed unless we admit that he was something of an authoritarian, we run the risk of overlooking those inner contradictions which make him such a complex, interesting, many-sided character.

Text

The student of Johnson's major political writings inevitably comes to learn a good deal about the author himself. They also contain some of Johnson's best prose, and for this reason alone it has seemed worthwhile to make them more readily accessible. The *Literary Magazine* is today a very rare book; while the four pamphlets comprising the bulk of this present volume have not been collected except in editions of Johnson's work since the author revised and published them in 1776 under the title *Political Tracts*. My text follows this edition, and only a few changes have been recorded in the notes.[1] Since the present volume is intended for the use of students of English, the original spelling and punctuation have been retained. Annotation has usually been given in note form. In providing a context for Johnson's numerous historical references, I have often had to be selective. For instance, many of the commonplaces of opposition cited in *The Patriot* may be found either in the newspapers of the period or (in a more sophisticated form) in James Burgh's *Political Disquisitions* (1774-5). Wherever possible use has been made of William Cobbett's *Parliamentary History*, and since allusion is so frequently made to

---

[1] For changes made in proof (some clearly at the request of the government) before *Taxation No Tyranny* originally appeared v. *Boswell's Life*, II. 313-15. The proof sheets from which Boswell here quotes are in the Hyde collection.

Introduction

Chatham, references to his speeches have been given some prominence. In other respects the notes, though spare, have been designed both to help the reader and to illustrate the variety of sources which Johnson had to draw on; yet they are in no sense intended as inclusive.

In my attempt to meet an early publication date, I have been generously supplied with advice and information by friends. In particular I wish to thank Dr. J. D. Fleeman, Professor D. J. Greene, Mr. C. G. Hardie, Dr. A. D. MacIntyre, Dr. L. F. Powell, Dr. Robert Shackleton, Mr. J. S. G. Simmons, and Mr. B. C. Southam.

J. P. H.

I

An Introduction to the Political State of Great-Britain

(1756)

As it is intended to exhibit in the following pamphlet an accurate account of every political debate, it appears necessary to lay before the reader a succinct account of British affairs, from the time in which our present relations to the continent began, and the competitions which keep us at variance with our neighbours arose. Without this previous knowledge, either recollected or acquired, it is not easy to understand the various opinions which every change in our affairs produces, or the questions which divide the nation into parties, and cause divisions in the parliament, and wars among the pamphleteers.

The present system of English politics may properly be said to have taken rise in the reign of queen Elizabeth. At this time the protestant religion was established, which naturally allied us to the reformed state, and made all the popish powers our enemies.

We began in the same reign to extend our trade, by which we made it necessary to ourselves to watch the commercial progress of our neighbours; and, if not to incommode and obstruct their traffick, to hinder them from impairing ours.

We then likewise settled colonies in America, which was become the great scene of European ambition; for, seeing with what treasures the Spaniards were annually inriched from Mexico and Peru, every nation imagined, that an American conquest or plantation would certainly fill the mother country with gold and silver. This produced a large extent of very distant dominions, of which we, at this time, neither knew nor foresaw the advantage or incumbrance: We seem to have snatched them into our hands, upon no very just principles of policy, only because every state, according to a prejudice of long continuance, concludes itself more powerful as its territories become larger.

The discoveries of new regions, which were then every day made, the profit of remote traffick, and the necessity of long voyages, produced, in a few years, a great multiplication of shipping. The sea was considered as the wealthy element; and, by degrees, a new kind of sovereignty arose, called naval dominion.

As the chief trade of the world, so the chief maritime power was at first in the hands of the Portuguese and Spaniards, who, by a compact, to which the consent of other princes was not asked, had divided the newly discovered countries between them; but the crown of Portugal having fallen to the king of Spain, or being seized by him, he was master of the ships of the two nations, with which he kept all the coasts of Europe in alarm, till the Armada, which he had raised at a vast expence for the conquest of England, was destroyed, which put a stop, and almost an end, to the naval power of the Spaniards.

At this time the Dutch, who were oppressed by the Spaniards, and feared yet greater evils than they felt, resolved no longer to endure the insolence of their masters: they therefore revolted, and after a struggle, in which they were assisted by the money and forces of Elizabeth, erected an independent and powerful commonwealth.

When the inhabitants of the Low-Countries had formed their system of government, and some remission of the war gave them leisure to form schemes of future prosperity, they easily perceived that, as their territories were narrow and their numbers small, they could preserve themselves only by that power which is the consequence of wealth; and that, by a people whose country produced only the necessaries of life, wealth was not to be acquired, but from foreign dominions, and by the transportation of the products of one country into another.

From this necessity, thus justly estimated, arose a plan of commerce, which was for many years prosecuted with industry and success, perhaps never seen in the world before, and by which the poor tenants of mudwalled villages and impassable bogs, erected themselves into high and mighty states, who put the greatest monarchs at defiance, whose alliance was courted by the proudest, and whose power was dreaded by the fiercest nation. By the establishment of this state there arose to England a new ally and a new rival.

At this time, which seems to be the period destined for the change of the face of Europe, France began first to rise into power, and, from defending her own provinces with difficulty and fluctuating success, to threaten her neighbours with incroachments and devastations. Henry the fourth having, after a long struggle, obtained the crown, found it easy to govern nobles exhausted and wearied with a long civil war, and having composed the disputes between the protestants and papists, so as to obtain, at least, a truce for both parties, was at leisure to accumulate treasure, and raise forces which he purposed to have employed in a design of settling for ever the balance of Europe. Of this great scheme he lived not to see the vanity, or to feel the disappointment; for he was murdered in the midst of his mighty preparations.

The French however were in this reign taught to know their own power; and the great designs of a king, whose wisdom they had so long experienced, even though they were not brought to actual experiment, disposed them to consider themselves as masters of the destiny of their neighbours; and, from that time, he that shall nicely examine their schemes and conduct will, I believe, find that they began to take an air of superiority, to which they had never pretended before; and that they have been always employed, more or less openly upon schemes of dominion, though with frequent interruptions from domestic troubles, and with those intermissions which human counsels must always suffer, as men intrusted with great affairs are dissipated in youth, and languid in age are embarrassed by competitors, or, without any external reason, change their minds.

France was now no longer in dread of insults and invasions from England. She was not only able to maintain her own territories, but prepared, on all occasions, to invade others, and we had now a neighbour whose interest it was to be an enemy, and who has disturbed us, from that time to this, with open hostility or secret machinations.

Such was the state of England and its neighbours, when Elizabeth left the crown to James of Scotland. It has not, I think, been frequently observed by historians at how critical a time the union of the two kingdoms happened. Had England and Scotland continued separate kingdoms, when France was established in the full possession of her natural power, the Scots, in continuance of the league, which it would now have been more than ever their interest to observe, would, upon every instigation of the French court, have raised an army with French money, and harrassed us with an invasion, in which they would have thought themselves successful, whatever numbers they might have left behind them. To a people warlike and indigent, an incursion into a rich country is never hurtful. The pay of France, and the plunder of the northern counties, would always have tempted them to hazard their lives, and we should have been under a necessity of keeping a line of garrisons along our border.

This trouble, however, we escaped by the accession of king James, but it is uncertain, whether his natural disposition did not injure us more than this accidental condition happened to benefit us. He was a man of great theoretical knowledge, but of no practical wisdom; he was very well able to discern the true interest of himself, his kingdom, and his posterity, but sacrificed it, upon all occasions, to his present pleasure or his present ease; so conscious of his own knowledge and abilities, that he would not suffer a minister to govern, and so lax of attention, and timorous of opposition, that he was not able to govern for himself. With this character James quietly saw the Dutch invade our commerce; the French grew every day stronger and stronger, and the protestant interest, of which he boasted himself the head, was oppressed on every side, while he writ, and hunted, and dispatched ambassadors, who, when their master's weakness was once known, were treated in foreign courts with very little ceremony. James, however, took care to be flattered at home, and was neither angry nor ashamed at the appearance that he made in other countries.

Thus England grew weaker, or what is in political estimation the same thing, saw her neighbours grow stronger, without receiving proportionable additions to her own power. Not that the mischief was so great as it is generally conceived or represented; for, I believe, it may be made to appear, that the wealth of the nation was, in this reign, very much increased, though that of the crown was lessened. Our reputation for war was impaired, but commerce seems to have been carried on with great industry and vigour, and nothing was wanting, but that we should have defended ourselves from the incroachments of our neighbours.

The inclination to plant colonies in America still continued, and this being the only project in which men of adventure and enterprise could exert their qualities in a pacific reign, multitudes, who were discontented with their condition in their native country, and such multitudes there will always be, sought relief, or at least change in the western regions, where they settled in the northern part of the continent, at a distance from the Spaniards at that time almost the only nation that had any power or will to obstruct us.

Such was the condition of this country when the unhappy Charles inherited the crown. He had seen the errors of his father, without being able to prevent them, and, when he began his reign, endeavoured to raise the nation to its former dignity. The French papists had begun a new war upon the protestants: Charles sent a fleet to invade Rhee and relieve Rochelle, but his attempts were defeated, and the protestants were subdued. The Dutch grown wealthy and strong, claimed the right of fishing in the British seas: this claim the king, who saw the increasing power of the states of Holland, resolved to contest. But for this end it was necessary to build a fleet, and a fleet could not be built without expence: he was advised to levy ship-money, which gave occasion to the civil war, of which the events and conclusion are too well known.

While the inhabitants of this island were embroiled among themselves, the power of France and Holland was every day increasing. The Dutch had overcome the difficulties of their infant commonwealth; and as they still retained their vigour and industry, from rich grew continually richer, and from powerful more powerful. They extended their traffick, and had not yet admitted luxury, so that they had the means and the will to accumulate wealth, without any incitement to spend it. The French, who wanted nothing to make them powerful, but a prudent regulation of their revenues, and a proper use of their natural advantages, by the successive care of skilful ministers became every day stronger, and more conscious of their strength.

About this time it was, that the French first began to turn their thoughts to traffick and navigation, and to desire like other nations an American territory. All the fruitful and valuable parts of the western world were already either occupied or claimed, and nothing remained for France but the leavings of other navigators, for she was not yet haughty enough to seize what the neighbouring powers had already appropriated.

The French therefore contented themselves with sending a colony to Canada, a cold uncomfortable uninviting region, from which nothing but furrs and fish were to be had, and where the new inhabitants could only pass a laborious and necessitous life in perpetual regret of the deliciousness and plenty of their native country.

Notwithstanding the opinion which our countrymen have been taught to entertain of the comprehension and foresight of French politicians, I am not able to persuade myself, that when this colony was first planted, it was thought of much value, even by those that encouraged it; there was probably nothing more intended than to provide a drain into which the waste of an exuberant nation might be thrown, a place where those who could do no good might live without the power of doing mischief. Some new advantage they undoubtedly saw, or imagined themselves to see, and what more was necessary to the establishment of the colony was supplied by natural inclination to experiments, and that impatience of doing nothing, to which mankind perhaps owe much of what is imagined to be effected by more splendid motives.

In this region of desolate sterility they settled themselves, upon whatever principle; and as they have from that time had the happiness of a government by which no interest has been neglected, nor any part of their subjects overlooked, they have, by continual encouragement and assistance from France, been perpetually enlarging their bounds and increasing their numbers.

These were at first, like other nations who invaded America, inclined to consider the neighbourhood of the natives, as troublesome and dangerous, and are charged with having destroy'd great numbers, but they are now grown wiser, if not honester, and instead of endeavouring to frighten the Indians away, they invite them to intermarriage and cohabitation, and allure them by all practicable methods to become the subjects of the king of France.

If the Spaniards, when they first took possession of the newly discovered world, instead of destroying the inhabitants by thousands, had either had the unanimity or the policy to have conciliated them by kind treatment, and to have united them gradually

An Introduction to the Political State of Great-Britain

to their own people, such an accession might have been made to the power of the king of Spain, as would have made him far the greatest monarch that ever yet ruled in the globe; but the opportunity was lost by foolishness and cruelty, and now can never be recovered.

When the parliament had finally prevailed over our king and the army over the parliament, the interest of the two commonwealths of England and Holland soon appeared to be opposite, and the new government declared war against the Dutch. In this contest was exerted the utmost power of the two nations, and the Dutch were finally defeated, yet not with such evidence of superiority as left us much reason to boast our victory; they were obliged however to solicit peace, which was granted them on easy conditions, and Cromwell, who was now possessed of the supreme power, was left at leisure to pursue other designs.

The European powers had not yet ceased to look with envy on the Spanish acquisitions in America, and therefore Cromwell thought that, if he gained any part of these celebrated regions, he should exalt his own reputation, and inrich the country. He therefore quarreled with the Spaniards upon some such subject of contention, as he that is resolved upon hostility may always find, and sent Pen and Venables into the western seas. They first landed in *Hispaniola*, whence they were driven off with no great reputation to themselves, and that they might not return without having done something, they afterwards invaded Jamaica, where they found less resistance, and obtained that Island, which was afterwards consigned to us, being probably of little value to the Spaniards, and continues to this day a place of great wealth and dreadful wickedness, a den of tyrants, and a dungeon of slaves.

Cromwell, who perhaps had not leisure to study foreign politics, was very fatally mistaken with regard to Spain and France. Spain had been the last power in Europe, which had openly pretended to give law to other nations, and the memory of this terror remained when the real cause was at an end. We had more lately been frighted by Spain than by France, and though very few were then alive of the generation that had their sleep broken by the Armada, yet the name of the Spaniards was still terrible, and a war against them was pleasing to the people.

Our own troubles had left us very little desire to look out upon the continent, and inveterate prejudice hindered us from perceiving, that for more than half a century the power of France had been increasing, and that of Spain had been growing less; nor does it seem to have been remembered, which, yet required no great depth of policy to discern, that of two monarchs, neither of which could be long our friend, it was our interest to have the weaker near us, or that if a war should happen, Spain, however wealthy or strong in herself, was by the dispersion of her territories more obnoxious to the attacks of a naval power, and consequently had more to fear from us, and had it less in her power to hurt us.

All these considerations were overlooked by the wisdom of that age, and Cromwell assisted the French to drive the Spaniards out of Flanders at a time when it was our interest to have supported the Spaniards against France, as formerly the Hollanders against Spain, by which we might at least have retarded the growth of the French power, though I think it must have finally prevailed.

During this time, our colonies which were less disturbed by our commotions than the mother country, naturally increased; it is probable that many who were unhappy at home took shelter in those remote regions, where for the sake of inviting greater numbers, every one was allowed to think and live his own way. The French settlement in the mean time went slowly forward, too inconsiderable to raise any jealousy, and too weak to attempt any incroachments.

When Cromwell died, the confusions that followed produced the restoration of monarchy, and some time was employed in repairing the ruins of our constitution, and restoring the nation to a state of peace. In every change there will be many that suffer real or imaginary grievances, and therefore many will be dissatisfied. This was, perhaps, the reason why several colonies had their beginning in the reign of Charles the second. The Quakers willingly sought refuge in Pensylvania; and it is not unlikely that Carolina owed its inhabitants to the remains of that restless disposition, which had given so much disturbance to our country, and had now no opportunity of acting at home.

The Dutch still continuing to increase in wealth and power, either kindled the resentment of their neighbours by their insolence, or raised their envy by their prosperity. Charles made war upon them without much advantage; but they were obliged at last

An Introduction to the Political State of Great-Britain

to confess him the sovereign of the narrow seas. They were reduced almost to extremities by an invasion from France; but soon recovered from their consternation, and, by the fluctuation of war, regained their cities and provinces with the same speed as they had lost them.

During the time of Charles the second the power of France was every day increasing; and Charles, who never disturbed himself with remote consequences, saw the progress of her arms, and the extension of her dominions, with very little uneasiness. He was indeed sometimes driven by the prevailing faction into confederacies against her; but as he had, probably, a secret partiality in her favour, he never persevered long in acting against her, nor ever acted with much vigour: so that, by his feeble resistance, he rather raised her confidence, than hindered her designs.

About this time the French first began to perceive the advantage of commerce, and the importance of a naval force; and such encouragement was given to manufactures, and so eagerly was every project received, by which trade could be advanced, that, in a few years, the sea was filled with their ships, and all the parts of the world crowded with their merchants. There is, perhaps, no instance in human story of such a change produced, in so short a time, in the schemes and manners of a people, of so many new sources of wealth opened, and such numbers of artificers and merchants made to start out of the ground, as was seen in the ministry of Colbert.

Now it was that the power of France became formidable to England. Her dominions were large before, and her armies numerous; but her operations were necessarily confined to the continent. She had neither ships for the transportation of her troops, nor money for their support in distant expeditions. Colbert saw both these wants, and saw that commerce only would supply them. The fertility of their country furnishes the French with commodities; the poverty of the common people keeps the price of labour low. By the obvious practice of selling much and buying little, it was apparent that they would soon draw the wealth of other countries into their own; and, by carrying out their merchandise in their own vessels, a numerous body of sailors would quickly be raised.

This was projected, and this was performed. The king of France was soon enabled to bribe those whom he could not conquer, and to terrify with his fleets those whom his armies could not have approached. The influence of France was suddenly diffused over all the globe; her arms were dreaded, and her pensions received in remote regions, and those were almost ready to acknowledge her sovereignty, who, a few years before, had scarcely heard her name. She thundered on the coasts of Africa, and received ambassadors from Siam.

So much may be done by one wise man, endeavouring with honesty the advantage of the public. But that we may not rashly condemn all ministers as wanting wisdom or integrity, whose counsels have produced no such apparent benefits to their country, it must be considered, that Colbert had means of acting, which our government does not allow. He could inforce all his orders by the power of an absolute monarch; he could compel individuals to sacrifice their private profit to the general good; he could make one understanding preside over many hands, and remove difficulties by quick and violent expedients. Where no man thinks himself under any obligation to submit to another, and, instead of co-operating in one great scheme, every one hastens through by-paths to private profit, no great change can suddenly be made; nor is superior knowledge of much effect, where every man resolves to use his own eyes and his own judgment, and every one applauds his own dexterity and diligence in proportion as he becomes rich sooner than his neighbour.

Colonies are always the effects and causes of navigation. They who visit many countries find some in which pleasure, profit or safety invite them to settle; and these settlements, when they are once made, must keep a perpetual correspondence with the original country, to which they are subject, and on which they depend for protection in danger, and supplies in necessity. So that a country, once discovered and planted, must always find employment for shipping, more certainly than any foreign commerce, which, depending on casualties, may be sometimes more and sometimes less, and which other nations may contract or suppress. A trade to colonies can never be much impaired, being, in reality, only an intercourse between distant provinces of the same empire, from which intruders are easily excluded; likewise the interest and affection of the correspondent parties, however distant, is the same.

On this reason all nations, whose power has been exerted on the ocean, have fixed colonies in remote parts of the world, and while those colonies subsisted, navigation, if it did not increase, was always preserved from total decay. With this policy the French were well acquainted, and therefore improved and augmented the settlements in America, and other regions, in proportion as they advanced their schemes of naval greatness.

The exact time in which they made their acquisitions in America, or other quarters of the globe, it is not necessary to collect. It is sufficient to observe, that their trade and their colonies increased together; and, if their naval armaments were carried on, as they really were, in greater proportion to their commerce, than can be practised in other countries, it must be attributed to the martial disposition at that time prevailing in the nation, to the frequent wars which Lewis the fourteenth made upon his neighbours, and to the extensive commerce of the English and Dutch, which afforded so much plunder to privateers, that war was more lucrative than traffick.

Thus the naval power of France continued to increase during the reign of Charles the second, who, between his fondness of ease and pleasure, the struggles of faction, which he could not suppress, and his inclination to the friendship of absolute monarchy, had not much power or desire to repress it. And of James the second, it could not be expected that he should act against his neighbours with great vigour, having the whole body of his subjects to oppose. He was not ignorant of the real interest of his country; he desired its power and its happiness, and thought rightly, that there is no happiness without religion; but he thought very erroneously and absurdly, that there is no religion without popery.

When the necessity of self-preservation had impelled the subjects of James to drive him from the throne, there came a time in which the passions, as well as interest of the government, acted against the French, and in which it may perhaps be reasonably doubted, whether the desire of humbling France was not stronger than that of exalting England; of this, however, it is not necessary to inquire, since, though the intention may be different, the event will be the same. All mouths were now open to declare what every eye had observed before, that the arms of France were become dangerous to Europe, and that, if her incroachments were suffered a little longer, resistance would be too late.

An Introduction to the Political State of Great-Britain

It was now determined to reassert the empire of the sea; but it was more easily determined than performed; the French made a vigorous defence against the united power of England and Holland, and were sometimes masters of the ocean, though the two maritime powers were united against them. At length, however, they were defeated at La Hogue; a great part of their fleet was destroyed, and they were reduced to carry on the war only with their privateers, from whom there was suffered much petty mischief, though there was no danger of conquest or invasion. They distressed our merchants, and obliged us to the continual expence of convoys and fleets of observation; and, by skulking in little coves and shallow waters, escaped our pursuit.

In this reign began our confederacy with the Dutch, which mutual interest has now improved into a friendship, conceived by some to be inseparable, and from that time the states began to be termed, in the stile of politicians, our faithful friends, the allies which nature has given us, our protestant confederates, and by many other names of national endearment. We have, it is true, the same interest, as opposed to France, and some resemblance of religion, as opposed to popery; but we have such a rivalry, in respect of commerce, as will always keep us from very close adherence to each other. No mercantile man, or mercantile nation, has any friendship but for money, and alliance between them will last no longer than their common safety or common profit is endangered; no longer than they have an enemy, who threatens to take from each more than either can steal from the other.

We were both sufficiently interested in repressing the ambition, and obstructing the commerce of France; and therefore we concurred with as much fidelity and as regular co-operation as is commonly found. The Dutch were in immediate danger, the armies of their enemies hovered over their country, and therefore they were obliged to dismiss for a time their love of money, and their narrow projects of private profit, and to do what a trader does not willingly at any time believe necessary, to sacrifice a part for the preservation of the whole.

A peace was at length made, and the French with their usual vigour and industry rebuilt their fleets, restored their commerce, and became in a very few years able to contest again the dominion of the sea. Their ships were well built, and always very numerously manned, their commanders having no hopes but from their bravery or their fortune, were resolute, and being very carefully educated for the sea, were eminently skilful.

All this was soon perceived, when queen Anne, the then darling of England, declared war against France. Our success by sea, though sufficient to keep us from dejection, was not such as dejected our enemies. It is, indeed, to be confessed, that we did not exert our whole naval strength; Marlborough was the governor of our counsels, and the great view of Marlborough was a war by land, which he knew well how to conduct, both to the honour of his country and his own profit. The fleet was therefore starved that the army might be supplied, and naval advantages were neglected for the sake of taking a town in Flanders, to be garrisoned by our allies. The French, however, were so weakened by one defeat after another, that, though their fleet was never destroyed by any total overthrow, they at last retained it in their harbours, and applied their whole force to the resistance of the confederate army, that now began to approach their frontiers, and threatened to lay waste their provinces and cities.

In the latter years of this war, the danger of their neighbourhood in America seems to have been considered, and a fleet was fitted out and supplied with a proper number of land forces to seize Quebec, the capital of Canada, or New France; but this expedition miscarried, like that of Anson against the Spaniards, by the lateness of the season, and our ignorance of the coasts, on which we were to act. We returned with loss, and only excited our enemies to greater vigilance, and perhaps to stronger fortifications.

When the peace of Utrecht was made, which those who clamoured among us most loudly against it, found it their interest to keep, the French applied themselves with the utmost industry to the extension of their trade, which we were so far from hindering, that for many years our ministry thought their friendship of such value, as to be cheaply purchased by whatever concession.

Instead therefore of opposing, as we had hitherto professed to do, the boundless ambition of the house of Bourbon, we became on a sudden solicitous for its exaltation and studious of its interest. We assisted the schemes of France and Spain with our fleets, and endeavoured to make these our friends by servility, whom nothing but power will keep quiet, and who must always be our enemies while they are endeavouring to grow greater, and we determine to remain free.

That nothing might be omitted which could testify our willingness to continue on any terms the good friends of France, we were content to assist not only their conquests but their traffick; and though we did not openly repeal the prohibitory laws, we yet tamely suffered commerce to be carried on between the two nations, and wool was daily imported to enable them to make cloth, which they carried to our markets and sold cheaper than we.

During all this time, they were extending and strengthening their settlements in America, contriving new modes of traffick, and framing new alliances with the Indian nations. They began now to find these northern regions barren and desolate as they are, sufficiently valuable to desire at least a nominal possession, that might furnish a pretence for the exclusion of others; they therefore extended their claim to tracts of land, which they could never hope to occupy, took care to give their dominions an unlimited magnitude, have given in their maps the name of Louisiana to a country, of which part is claimed by the Spaniards, and part by the English, without any regard to ancient boundaries or prior discovery.

When the return of Columbus from his great voyage had filled all Europe with wonder and curiosity, Henry the seventh sent Sebastain Cabot to try what could be found for the benefit of England: he declined the track of Columbus, and, steering to the westward, fell upon the island, which, from that time, was called by the English, Newfoundland. Our princes seem to have considered themselves as intitled by their right of prior seizure to the northern parts of America, as the Spaniards were allowed by universal consent their claim to the southern region for the same reason, and we accordingly made our principal settlements within the limits of our own discoveries, and, by degrees, planted the eastern coast from Newfoundland to Georgia.

As we had, according to the European principles which allow nothing to the natives of these regions, our choice of situation in this extensive country, we naturally fixed our habitations along the coast, for the sake of traffick and correspondence, and all the conveniencies of navigable rivers. And when one port or river was occupied, the next colony, instead of fixing themselves in the inland parts behind the former, went on southward, till they pleased themselves with another maritime situation. For this reason our colonies have more length than depth; their extent from east to west, or from the sea to the interior country, bears no proportion to their reach along the coast from north to south.

It was, however, understood, by a kind of tacit compact among the commercial powers, that possession of the coast included a right to the inland; and, therefore, the charters granted to the several colonies limit their districts only from north to south, leaving their possessions from east to west unlimited and discretional, supposing that, as the colony increases, they may take lands as they shall want them, the possession of the coasts excluding other navigators, and the unhappy Indians having no right of nature or of nations.

This right of the first European possessor was not disputed till it became the interest of the French to question it. Canada or New-France, on which they made their first settlement, is situated eastward of our colonies, between which they pass up the great river of St. Laurence, with Newfoundland on the north, and Nova Scotia on the south. Their establishment in this country was neither envied nor hindered, and they lived here, in no great numbers a long time, neither molesting their European neighbours, nor molested by them.

But when they grew stronger and more numerous, they began to extend their territories; and, as it is natural for men to seek their own convenience, the desire of more fertile and agreeable habitations tempted them southward. There is land enough to the north and west of their settlements, which they may occupy with as good right as can be shewn by the other European usurpers, and which neither the English nor Spaniards will contest; but of this cold region they have enough already, and their resolution was to get a better country. This was not to be had but by settling to the west of our plantations, on ground which has been hitherto supposed to belong to us.

Hither, therefore, they resolved to remove, and to fix, at their own discretion, the western border of our colonies, which was heretofore considered as unlimited. Thus by forming a line of forts, in some measure parallel to the coast, they inclose us between their garrisons and the sea, and not only hinder our extension westward, but, whenever they have a sufficient navy in the sea, can harrass us on each side, as they can invade us, at pleasure, from one or other of their forts.

This design was not perhaps discovered as soon as it was formed, and was certainly not opposed so soon as it was discovered; we foolishly hoped, that their incroachments would stop, that they would be prevailed on by treaty and remonstrance, to give up what they had taken, or to put limits to themselves. We suffered them to establish one settlement after another, to pass boundary after boundary, and add fort to fort, till at last they grew strong enough to avow their designs, and defy us to obstruct them.

By these provocations long continued, we are at length forced into a war, in which we have had hitherto very ill fortune. Our troops under Braddock were dishonourably defeated; our fleets have yet done nothing more than take a few merchant-ships, and have distressed some private families, but have very little weakened the power of France. The detention of their seamen makes it indeed less easy for them to fit out their navy; but this deficiency will be easily supplied by the alacrity of the nation, which is always eager for war.

It is unpleasing to represent our affairs to our own disadvantage; yet it is necessary to shew the evils which we desire to be removed; and, therefore, some account may very properly be given of the measures which have given them their present superiority.

They are said to be supplied from France with better governors than our colonies have the fate to obtain from England. A French governor is seldom chosen for any other reason than his qualifications for his trust. To be a bankrupt at home, or to be so infamously vicious that he cannot be decently protected in his own country, seldom recommends any man to the government of a French colony. Their officers are commonly skilful either in war or commerce, and are taught to have no expectation of honour or preferment, but from the justice and vigour of their administration.

Their great security is the friendship of the natives, and to this advantage they have certainly an indubitable right; because it is the consequence of their virtue. It is ridiculous to imagine, that the friendship of nations, whether civil or barbarous, can be gained and kept but by kind treatment; and surely they who

An Introduction to the Political State of Great-Britain

intrude, uncalled, upon the country of a distant people, ought to consider the natives as worthy of common kindness, and content themselves to rob without insulting them. The French, as has been already observed, admit the Indians, by intermarriage, to an equality with themselves, and those nations, with which they have no such near intercourse, they gain over to their interest by honesty in their dealings. Our factors and traders having no other purpose in view than immediate profit, use all the arts of an *European* counting-house, to defraud the simple hunter of his furs.

These are some of the causes of our present weakness; our planters are always quarreling with their governor, whom they consider as less to be trusted than the French; and our traders hourly alienate the Indians by their tricks and oppressions, and we continue every day to shew by new proofs, that no people can be great who have ceased to be virtuous.

2

Observations on His Britannic Majesty's Treaties with Her Imperial Majesty of All the Russias and the Landgrave of Hesse-Cassel
(*1756*)

These are the treaties which for many months filled the senate with debates, and the kingdom with clamours, which were represented on one part as instances of the most profound policy and the most active care of the public welfare, and on the other, as acts of the most contemptible folly and most flagrant corruption, as violations of the great trust of government, by which the wealth of Britain is sacrificed to private views and to a particular province.

What honours our ministers and negotiators may expect to be paid to their wisdom it is hard to determine, for the demands of vanity are not easily estimated. They should consider before they call too loudly for encomiums, that they live in an age when the power of gold is no longer a secret, and in which no man finds much difficulty in making a bargain with money in his hand. To hire troops is very easy to those who are willing to pay their price. It appears therefore that whatever has been done was done by means which every man knows how to use if fortune is kind enough to put them in his power. To arm the nations of the north in the cause of Britain, to bring down hosts against France from the polar circle has indeed a sound of magnificence, which might induce a mind unacquainted with public affairs to imagine that some effort of policy more than human had been exerted, by which distant nations were armed in our defence, and the influence of Britain was extended to the utmost limits of the world. But when this striking phenomenon of negotiation is more nearly inspected, it appears a bargain merely mercantile of one power that wanted troops more than money, with another that wanted money, and was burdened with troops, between whom their mutual wants made an easy contract, and who have no other friendship for each other, than reciprocal convenience happens to produce.

We shall therefore leave the praises of our ministers to others, yet not without this acknowledgment, that if they have done little, they do not seem to boast of doing much, and that whether instructed by modesty or frugality, they have not wearied the public with mercenary panegyrists, but have been content with the concurrence of the parliament, and have not much solicited the applauses of the people.

In public as in private transactions men more frequently deviate from the right for want of virtue than of wisdom; and those who declare themselves dissatisfied with these treaties impute them not to folly but corruption.

By these advocates for the independence of Britain, who, whether their arguments be just or not, seem to be most favourably heard by the people, it is alleged, that these treaties are expensive without advantage, that they waste the treasure, which we want for our own defence, upon a foreign interest, and pour the gains of our commerce into the coffers of princes, whose enmity cannot hurt nor friendship help us, who set their subjects to sale like sheep or oxen without any enquiry after the intentions of the buyer, and will withdraw the troops with which they have supplied us, whenever a higher bidder shall be found.

This perhaps is true, but whether it be true or false is not worth enquiry. We did not expect to buy their friendship but their troops; nor did we examine upon what principle we were supplied with assistance, it was sufficient that we wanted forces, and that they were willing to furnish them. Policy never pretended to make men wise and good, the utmost of her power is to make the best use of men such as they are, to lay hold on lucky hours, to watch the present wants and present interests of others, and make them subservient to her own convenience.

It is farther urged with great vehemence, that these troops of Russia and Hesse are not hired in defence of Britain; that we are engaged in a naval war for territories on a distant continent, and that these troops though mercenaries can never be auxiliaries; that they increase the burden of the war without hastening its conclusion, or promoting its success; since they can neither be sent into America, the only part of the world where England can, on the present occasion, have any employment for land forces, nor be put into our ships, by which and by which only we are now to oppose and subdue our enemies.

Nature has stationed us in an island inaccessible but by sea, and we are now at war with an enemy, whose naval power is inferior to our own, and from whom therefore we are in no danger of invasion: to what purpose then are troops hired in such uncommon numbers? To what end do we procure strength which we cannot exert, and exhaust the nation with subsidies at a time when nothing is disputed, which the princes who receive our subsidies can defend. If we had purchased ships and hired seamen, we had apparently increased our power, and made ourselves formidable to our enemies, and, if any increase of security be possible, had secured ourselves still better from invasions: but what can the regiments of Russia or of Hesse contribute to the defence of the coasts of England, or by what assistance can they repay us the sums which we have stipulated to pay for their costly friendship?

The King of Great-Britain has indeed a territory on the continent, of which the natives of this island scarcely knew the name till the present family was call'd to the throne, and yet know little more than that our king visits it from time to time. Yet for the defence of this country are these subsidies apparently paid, and these troops evidently levied. The riches of our nation are sent into distant countries, and the strength which should be employed in our own quarrel consequently impaired, for the sake of dominions the interest of which has no connection with ours, and which by the act of succession we took care to keep separate from the British kingdoms.

To this the advocates for the subsidies say, that unreasonable stipulations, whether in the act of settlement or any other contract, are in themselves void, and that if a country connected with England by subjection to the same Sovereign is endangered by an English quarrel, it must be defended by English force, and that we do not engage in a war for the sake of Hanover, but that Hanover is for our sake exposed to danger.

Observations on his Britannic Majesty's Treaties

Those who brought in these foreign troops have still something further to say in their defence, and of no honest plea is it our intention to defraud them. They grant, that the terror of invasion may possibly be groundless, that the French may want the power or the courage to attack us in our own country; but they maintain likewise that an invasion is possible, that the armies of France are so numerous that she may hazard a large body on the ocean, without leaving herself exposed: that she is exasperated to the utmost degree of acrimony, and would be willing to do us mischief at her own peril. They allow that the invaders may be intercepted at sea, or that, if they land, they may be defeated by our native troops. But they say, and say justly, that danger is better avoided than encountered; that those ministers consult more the good of their country who prevent invasion, than repel it, and that if these auxiliaries have only saved us from the anxiety of expecting an enemy at our doors, or from the tumult and distress which an invasion, how soon soever repressed, would have produced, the public money is not spent in vain.

These arguments are admitted by some, and by others rejected. But even those that admit them, can admit them only as pleas of necessity, for they consider the reception of mercenaries into our country as the desperate remedy of desperate distress, and think with great reason, that all means of prevention should be tried to save us from any second need of such doubtful succours.

That we are able to defend our own country, that arms are most safely intrusted to our own hands, and that we have strength, and skill, and courage equal to the best of the nations of the continent, is the opinion of every Englishman who can think without prejudice, and speak without influence, and therefore it will not be easy to persuade the nation, a nation long renowned for valour, that it can need the help of foreigners to defend it from invasion. We have been long without the need of arms by our good fortune, and long without the use by our negligence, so long that the practice and almost the name of our old trained-bands is forgotten. But the story of ancient times will tell us, that the trained-bands were once able to maintain the quiet and safety of their country, and reason without history will inform us, that those men are most likely to fight bravely, or at least to fight obstinately, who fight for their own houses and farms, for their own wives and children.

Observations on his Britannic Majesty's Treaties

A bill was therefore offered for the prevention of any future danger or invasion, or necessity of mercenary forces, by re-establishing and improving the militia. It was passed by the Commons, but rejected by the Lords. That this bill, the first essay of political consideration as a subject long forgotten, should be liable to objection cannot be strange, but surely, justice, policy, common reason require that we should be trusted with our own defence, and be kept no longer in such a helpless state as at once to dread our enemies and confederates.

By the bill, such as it was formed, sixty thousand men would always be in arms . . . [who] may be upon any exigence easily increased to an hundred and fifty thousand, and I believe, neither our friends nor enemies will think it proper to insult our coasts when they expect to find upon them an hundred and fifty thousand Englishmen with swords in their hands.

3
Observations on the Present State of Affairs
(1756)

The time is now come in which every Englishman expects to be informed of the national affairs, and in which he has a right to have that expectation gratified. For whatever may be urged by ministers, or those whom vanity or interest make the followers of ministers, concerning the necessity of confidence in our governors, and the presumption of prying with profane eyes into the recesses of policy, it is evident, that this reverence can be claimed only by counsels yet unexecuted, and projects suspended in deliberation. But when a design has ended in miscarriage or success, when every eye and every ear is witness to general discontent, or general satisfaction, it is then a proper time to disintangle confusion and illustrate obscurity, to shew by what causes every event was produced, and in what effects it is likely to terminate: to lay down with distinct particularity what rumour always huddles in general exclamations, or perplexes by undigested narratives; to shew whence happiness or calamity is derived, and whence it may be expected, and honestly to lay before the people what inquiry can gather of the past, and conjecture can estimate of the future.

The general subject of the present war is sufficiently known. It is allowed on both sides, that hostilities began in America, and that the French and English quarrelled about the boundaries of their settlements, about grounds and rivers to which, I am afraid, neither can shew any other right than that of power, and which neither can occupy but by usurpation, and the dispossession of the natural lords and original inhabitants. Such is the contest that no honest man can heartily wish success to either party.

It may indeed be alleged, that the Indians have granted large tracts of land both to one and to the other; but these grants can add little to the validity of our titles, till it be experienced how they were obtained: for if they were extorted by violence, or induced by fraud; by threats, which the miseries of other nations had shewn not to be vain, or by promises of which no performance was ever intended, what are they but new modes of usurpation, but new instances of cruelty and treachery?

And indeed what but false hope, or restless terror can prevail upon a weaker nation to invite a stronger into their country, to give their lands to strangers whom no affinity of manners, or similitude of opinion can be said to recommend, to permit them to build towns from which the natives are excluded, to raise fortresses by which they are intimidated, to settle themselves with such strength, that they cannot afterwards be expelled, but are for ever to remain the masters of the original inhabitants, the dictators of their conduct, and the arbiters of their fate?

When we see men acting thus against the precepts of reason, and the instincts of nature, we cannot hesitate to determine, that by some means or other they were debarred from choice; that they were lured or frighted into compliance; that they either granted only what they found impossible to keep, or expected advantages upon the faith of their new inmates, which there was no purpose to confer upon them. It cannot be said, that the Indians originally invited us to their coasts; we went uncalled and unexpected to nations who had no imagination that the earth contained any inhabitants so distant and so different from themselves. We astonished them with our ships, with our arms, and with our general superiority. They yielded to us as to beings of another and higher race, sent among them from some unknown regions, with power which naked Indians could not resist, and which they were therefore, by every act of humility, to propitiate, that they, who could so easily destroy, might be induced to spare.

To this influence, and to this only, are to be attributed all the cessions and submissions of the Indian princes, if indeed any such cessions were ever made, of which we have no witness but those who claim from them, and there is no great malignity in suspecting, that those who have robbed have also lied.

Some colonies indeed have been established more peaceably than others. The utmost extremity of wrong has not always been

Observations on the Present State of Affairs

practised; but those that have settled in the new world on the fairest terms, have no other merit than that of a scrivener who ruins in silence over a plunderer that seizes by force; all have taken what had other owners, and all have had recourse to arms, rather than quit the prey on which they had fastened.

The American dispute between the French and us is therefore only the quarrel of two robbers for the spoils of a passenger, but as robbers have terms of confederacy, which they are obliged to observe as members of the gang, so the English and French may have relative rights, and do injustice to each other, while both are injuring the Indians. And such, indeed, is the present contest: they have parted the northern continent of America between them, and are now disputing about their boundaries, and each is endeavouring the destruction of the other by the help of the Indians, whose interest it is that both should be destroyed.

Both nations clamour with great vehemence about infraction of limits, violation of treaties, open usurpation, insidious artifices, and breach of faith. The English rail at the perfidious French, and the French at the encroaching English; they quote treaties on each side, charge each other with aspiring to universal monarchy, and complain on either part of the insecurity of possession near such turbulent neighbours.

Through this mist of controversy it can raise no wonder, that the truth is not easily discovered. When a quarrel has been long carried on between individuals, it is often very hard to tell by whom it was begun. Every fact is darkened by distance, by interest, and by multitudes. Information is not easily procured from far; those whom the truth will not favour, will not step voluntarily forth to tell it, and where there are many agents, it is easy for every single action to be concealed.

All these causes concur to the obscurity of the question, by whom were hostilities in America commenced? Perhaps there never can be remembered a time in which hostilities had ceased. Two powerful colonies enflamed with immemorial rivalry, and placed out of the superintendence of the mother nations, were not likely to be long at rest. Some opposition was always going forward, some mischief was every day done or meditated, and the borderers were always better pleased with what they could snatch from their neighbours, than what they had of their own.

Observations on the Present State of Affairs

In this disposition to reciprocal invasion a cause of dispute never could be wanting. The forests and desarts of America are without land-marks, and therefore cannot be particularly specified in stipulations; the appellations of those wide extended regions have in every mouth a different meaning, and are understood on either side as inclination happens to contract or extend them. Who has yet pretended to define how much of America is included in Brazil, Mexico, or Peru? It is almost as easy to divide the Atlantic ocean by a line, as clearly to ascertain the limits of those uncultivated, uninhabitable, unmeasured regions.

It is likewise to be considered, that contracts concerning boundaries are often left vague and indefinite without necessity, by the desire of each party, to interpret the ambiguity to its own advantage when a fit opportunity shall be found. In forming stipulations, the commissaries are often ignorant, and often negligent; they are sometimes weary with debate, and contract a tedious discussion into general terms, or refer it to a former treaty, which was never understood. The weaker part is always afraid of requiring explanations, and the stronger always has an interest in leaving the question undecided: thus it will happen without great caution on either side, that after long treaties solemnly ratified, the rights that had been disputed are still equally open to controversy.

In America it may easily be supposed, that there are tracts of land yet claimed by neither party, and therefore mentioned in no treaties, which yet one or the other may be afterwards inclined to occupy; but to these vacant and unsettled countries each nation may pretend, as each conceives itself intitled to all that is not expressly granted to the other.

Here then is a perpetual ground of contest, every enlargement of the possessions of either will be considered as something taken from the other, and each will endeavour to regain what had never been claimed, but that the other occupied it.

Thus obscure in its original is the American contest. It is difficult to find the first invader, or to tell where invasion properly begins; but I suppose it is not to be doubted, that after the last war, when the French had made peace with such apparent superiority, they naturally began to treat us with less respect in distant parts of the world, and to consider us as a people from whom they had nothing to fear, and who could no longer presume to contravene their designs, or to check their progress.

The power of doing wrong with impunity seldom waits long for the will, and it is reasonable to believe, that in America the French would avow their purpose of aggrandising themselves with at least as little reserve as in Europe. We may therefore readily believe, that they were unquiet neighbours, and had no great regard to right which they believed us no longer able to enforce.

That in forming a line of forts behind our colonies, if in no other part of their attempt, they had acted against the general intention, if not against the literal terms of treaties, can scarcely be denied; for it never can be supposed, that we intended to be inclosed between the sea and the French garrisons, or preclude ourselves from extending our plantations backwards to any length that our convenience should require.

With dominion is conferred every thing that can secure dominion. He that has the coast, has likewise the sea to a certain distance; he that possesses a fortress, has the right of prohibiting another fortress to be built within the command of its cannon. When therefore we planted the coast of North-America we supposed the possession of the inland region granted to an indefinite extent, and every nation that settled in that part of the world seems, by the permission of every other nation, to have made the same supposition in its own favour.

Here then, perhaps, it will be safest to fix the justice of our cause; here we are apparently and indisputably injured, and this injury may, according to the practice of nations, be justly resented. Whether we have not in return made some incroachments upon them, must be left doubtful, till our practices on the Ohio shall be stated and vindicated. There are no two nations confining on each other, between whom a war may not always be kindled with plausible pretences on either part, as there is always passing between them a reciprocation of injuries and fluctuation of incroachments.

From the conclusion of the last peace perpetual complaints of the supplantations and invasions of the French have been sent to Europe from our colonies, and transmitted to our ministers at Paris, where good words were sometimes given us, and the

Observations on the Present State of Affairs

practices of the American commanders were sometimes disowned, but no redress was ever obtained, nor is it probable that any prohibition was sent to America. We were still amused with such doubtful promises as those who are afraid of war are ready to interpret in their own favour, and the French pushed forward their line of fortresses, and seemed to resolve that before our complaints were finally dismissed, all remedy should be hopeless.

We likewise endeavour'd at the same time to form a barrier against the Canadians by sending a colony to New-Scotland, a cold uncomfortable tract of ground, of which we had long the nominal possession before we really began to occupy it. To this those were invited whom the cessation of war deprived of employment, and made burdensom to their country, and settlers were allured thither by many fallacious descriptions of fertile vallies and clear skies. What effect these pictures of American happiness had upon my countrymen I was never informed, but I suppose very few sought provision in those frozen regions, whom guilt or poverty did not drive from their native country. About the boundaries of this new colony there were some disputes, but as there was nothing yet worth a contest, the power of the French was not much exerted on that side: some disturbance was however given and some skirmishes ensued. But perhaps being peopled chiefly with soldiers, who would rather live by plunder than by agriculture, and who consider war as their best trade, New-Scotland would be more obstinately defended than some settlements of far greater value, and the French are too well informed of their own interest, to provoke hostility for no advantage, or to select that country for invasion, where they must hazard much, and can win little. They therefore pressed on southward behind our ancient and wealthy settlements, and built fort after fort at such distances that they might conveniently relieve one another, invade our colonies with sudden incursions, and retire to places of safety before our people could unite to oppose them.

This design of the French has been long formed, and long known, both in America and Europe, and might at first have been easily repressed had force been used instead of expostulation. When the English attempted a settlement upon the island of St. Lucia, the French, whether justly or not, considering it as neutral and forbidden to be occupied by either nation, immediately landed

Observations on the Present State of Affairs

upon it, and destroyed the houses, wasted the plantations, and drove or carried away the inhabitants. This was done in the time of peace, when mutual professions of friendship were daily exchanged by the two courts, and was not considered as any violation of treaties, nor was any more than a very soft remonstrance made on our part.

The French therefore taught us how to act, but an Hanoverian quarrel with the house of Austria for some time induced us to court, at any expence, the alliance of a nation whose very situation makes them our enemies. We suffered them to destroy our settlements, and to advance their own, which we had an equal right to attack. The time however came at last, when we ventured to quarrel with Spain, and then France no longer suffered the appearance of peace to subsist between us, but armed in defence of her ally.

The events of the war are well known, we pleased ourselves with a victory at Dettingen, where we left our wounded men to the care of our enemies, but our army was broken at Fontenoy and Val; and though after the disgrace which we suffered in the Mediterranean we had some naval success, and an accidental dearth made peace necessary for the French, yet they prescribed the conditions, obliged us to give hostages, and acted as conquerors, though as conquerors of moderation.

In this war the Americans distinguished themselves in a manner unknown and unexpected. The New English raised an army, and under the command of Pepperel took Cape-Breton, with the assistance of the fleet. This is the most important fortress in America. We pleased ourselves so much with the acquisition, that we could not think of restoring it, and among the arguments used to inflame the people against Charles Stuart, it was very clamorously urged, that if he gained the kingdom, he would give Cape-Breton back to the French.

The French however had a more easy expedient to regain Cape-Breton than by exalting Charles Stuart to the English throne, they took in their turn fort St. George, and had our East-India company wholly in their power, whom they restored at the peace to their former possessions, that they may continue to export our silver.

Cape-Breton therefore was restored, and the French were

re-established in America, with equal power and greater spirit, having lost nothing by the war which they had before gained.

To the general reputation of their arms, and that habitual superiority which they derive from it, they owe their power in America, rather than to any real strength, or circumstances of advantage. Their numbers are yet not great; their trade, though daily improved, is not very extensive; their country is barren, their fortresses, though numerous, are weak, and rather shelters from wild beasts, or savage nations, than places built for defence against bombs or cannons. Cape-Breton has been found not to be impregnable; nor, if we consider the state of the places possessed by the two nations in America, is there any reason upon which the French should have presumed to molest us; but that they thought our spirit so broken that we durst not resist them, and in this opinion our long forbearance easily confirmed them.

We forgot, or rather avoided to think, that what we delayed to do must be done at last, and done with more difficulty, as it was delayed longer; that while we were complaining, and they were eluding, or answering our complaints, fort was rising upon fort, and one invasion made a precedent for another.

This confidence of the French is exalted by some real advantages. If they possess in those countries less than we, they have more to gain, and less to hazard; if they are less numerous, they are better united.

The French compose one body with one head. They have all the same interest, and agree to pursue it by the same means. They are subject to a governor commission'd by an absolute monarch, and participating the authority of his master. Designs are therefore formed without debate, and executed without impediment. They have yet more martial than mercantile ambition, and seldom suffer their military schemes to be entangled with collateral projects of gain: they have no wish but for conquest, of which they justly consider riches as the consequence.

Some advantages they will always have as invaders. They make war at the hazard of their enemies: the contest being carried on in our territories we must lose more by a victory than they will suffer by a defeat. They will subsist, while they stay, upon our plantations, and perhaps destroy them when they can stay no longer. If we pursue them and carry the war into their dominions, our difficulties will encrease every step as we advance, for we shall leave plenty behind us, and find nothing in Canada, but lakes and forests barren and trackless, our enemies will shut themselves up in their forts, against which it is difficult to bring cannon through so rough a country, and which if they are provided with good magazines will soon starve those who besiege them.

All these are the natural effects of their government, and situation; they are accidentally more formidable as they are less happy. But the favour of the Indians which they enjoy, with very few exceptions, among all the nations of the northern continent, we ought to consider with other thoughts; this favour we might have enjoyed, if we had been careful to deserve it. The French by having these savage nations on their side, are always supplied with spies, and guides, and with auxiliaries, like the Tartars to the Turks or the Hussars to the Germans, of no great use against troops ranged in order of battle, but very well qualified to maintain a war among woods and rivulets, where much mischief may be done by unexpected onsets, and safety be obtained by quick retreats. They can waste a colony by sudden inroads, surprise the straggling planters, frighten the inhabitants into towns, hinder the cultivation of lands, and starve those whom they are not able to conquer.

4
Observations
(1758)

August 19

Our troops have at last taken a French town; Cherbourg is in the possession of the English. To celebrate a conquest of no small importance with any ostentation of triumph, would be ridiculous; but it is no less unreasonable to repress the joy which the gleam of success naturally gives, after a long continuance of the clouds of disappointment. This is the first attempt by which all has been done which was expected or desired, and from this we may hope for more advantages. Victory naturally produces elation of spirit, and elation reciprocally invites enterprize, and ensures victory.

It may be asked by those who affect, for some reason or other, to despise all the schemes of the Government, what we propose to gain by invading France with seven thousand men; a force which, to a Nation so numerous and warlike, must appear contemptible as a troop of wolves descending from the mountains? It may be asked, why we take a town which we cannot keep, and land only to embark again?

To all this, the answer is easy. We invade the French not to conquer, but to harrass and alarm them. We do not suppose that we put Paris or Versailles in any immediate terror, but we know that the Maritime Provinces are kept in perpetual disturbance, and distraction; that wherever we land the inhabitants are distressed by their fears, if not by their sufferings. The distress of one part is not felt without inconvenience to the rest, and inconvenience long continued will make a people weary of war.

By taking and quitting, at pleasure, the towns of France, we convince all Europe of our naval superiority; we shew to other

Observations (August–September 1758)

Nations that the French have no fleets that can oppose us on the sea, and to the French themselves, that thay have no troops that can guard the coast. We diminish the reputation of the French for ever among Foreigners, and of the French Government among the French themselves. We destroy that prejudice which gave every petty people courage to treat us with contempt at the beginning of the War. Those Nations that, two years ago, saw us trembling at home, and calling out for succour from the Continent to protect us from an invasion, which it must always be remembred, the French had neither power nor design to execute, now see us insulting the coast of France, not only without repulse, but without resistance. We have had indeed no opportunity to exert our valour nor can boast of no routed armies, but that we ravage the country unopposed, if it does not give any new specimen of English courage, gives at least a proof of the weakness of France.

August 26

It is natural to pass from dejection to exultation. He that thought his danger more than it was, will set more value than he ought upon every glimpse of deliverance. When we lost Minorca a general panick fell upon the Nation, and every man met his neighbour with a clouded forehead, and a down cast eye, as if London had been besieged. Louisbourg is now taken, and our streets echo with triumph, and blaze with illumination, as if our King was once more proclaimed at Paris. Surprizes both of grief and joy are natural, but let us recover from them as soon as we can, and estimate every event according to its importance, and every acquisition according to its value. The siege of Louisbourg has been so happily conducted, that perhaps there are few examples in history of a place so strong, conquered in so short a time, with so little loss. Whether this facility of success be attributed to English skill, or to French timidity, it is equally pleasing. If our military skill be great, we may hope to conquer men who, tho' they have equal bravery, have less knowledge; if our enemies be timorous, they can never be formidable whatever be their skill. The French seem to have placed too much confidence in their ships, which made the harbour inaccessible by sea, and which they did not consider that the besiegers might destroy by their

Observations (August–September 1758)

batteries. Human caution is never able to guard all sides, and danger, when it comes unexpected, comes with double force. When the French saw their ships destroyed by shot from the land, they lost their courage, and forgot that their walls were yet undemolished. Thus Louisbourg was taken and the reputation of our arms restored, which is indeed one great effect, if not the greatest of this boasted conquest. Louisbourg is not useful to us, in the same degree as its loss is detrimental to our enemies. They value it as a port of security for their ships, as the place where their American forces may safely assemble, sheltered alike from hostilities and tempests. We can desire it only that we may deprive them of an advantageous station, for we do not want ports in that part of the world; so that much is taken from our enemies, but little gained to ourselves. But this is the condition of war; to make one part weaker, is to strengthen the other; and this advantage we have obtained not only by the capture of the fortress, but by the destruction of 11 ships, by which the French navy that was weak from the beginning of the war, is reduced to a state in which it can no longer hope to oppose us.

September 2

Since the siege of Olmutz was raised, there is little mention of the King of Prussia; we know only that he is retreating to his own dominions, and that the Austrian provinces are in some measure delivered from the terrors of the sword, and the burthen of contributions. Our fears are again returning upon us, and whenever the affairs of the Continent are mentioned, the King of Prussia is commiserated as a Potentate upon whom Destruction is opening her jaws, upon whose dominions all the surrounding Powers are bursting at once, and whose provinces are already allotted to his enemies. That he has indeed enemies on all sides is evident, but his enemies have greater names than forces. He has little to fear except from the Austrians, and from them he has not suffered much. It seems to have been the expectation of his English Allies, that his troops should conquer whatever they invade, that his name should disarm every hand that was raised against him; that he should pass without obstruction from province to province, and from city to city; that he should do all, and his enemies do nothing.

Observations (August–September 1758)

Elated with this hope, contrary to reason, contrary to experience, we saw him enter the field, expecting that every day would produce new acquisitions; and since we have seen his first enterprize fail of success, we descend at once from our elevation, consider miscarriage as an overthrow, and resign our hero to Death or Captivity. But what has happened to the King of Prussia, which does not happen to the most successful generals? He besieged a city, his ammunition was intercepted, he could not batter it without bullets, and therefore raised the siege. He was advancing into the enemies provinces, and encountered little opposition; his territories are invaded on the other side, and he finds it necessary to post his army nearer the center. The gain of a battle would reestablish him in his former superiority, and convince us once more that he is invincible; but perhaps he may think a battle too hazardous in his present situation, when his enemies are all so near him, and so ready to improve any advantage which he might give them by suffering a defeat. The truth is, that a battle is scarcely to be expected unless the King of Prussia should snatch some casual opportunity, or should be so confined on all sides as to find himself obliged to force open a passage; for the condition of the Austrians, after so many losses, is likewise such, that they cannot suffer another overthrow, without the utmost danger and distress. It is therefore not unlikely, that the remaining part of the summer will be spent in marches and counter-marches, excursions into the open country, and petty skirmishes of small parties.

September 9

Every public act either raises or sinks the honour of a people, and is therefore a proper subject of praise or reprehension. The pomp with which a few French colours were, on Wednesday, carried to St. Paul's, since perhaps it was very little considered before the exhibition may be fitly reviewed after it.

To celebrate victories by Triumphs, to notify, by some publick festivity, the happy success of military enterprizes, has been the practice of all civilized nations. State-craft has sometimes inverted this practice, and the people have been taught to rejoice when the army has been defeated. This is the grossest stratagem

Observations (August–September 1758)

of political fraud; and this, I hope, our Governors will never be reduced to practise; but some approaches to it are made, when we are taught to think our acquisitions greater than they are, or to express our joy in a manner disproportionate to the sorrow felt by our enemies.

The display of these captive colours, if not a Triumph, was at least an *Ovation,* and was to be understood by the gazing populace as an undoubted proof of the inferiority of France. But what has France yet suffered from the British arms, or what did we gain but the Colours, when these Colours fell into our hands? When the Trophies of Blenheim were displayed, one spectator was able to tell another, that the French were driven out of the Empire, and had lost, perhaps three hundred miles of territory; when the Spoils of Ramillies were carried thro' the city, it might have been truly proclaimed, that Flanders lay open to our army. But how were these Colours got, whence did they come, and what did they cost? They were not gained by a decisive victory; there is no army defeated, France is not much weaker than she was before, and the war, however successful, is not much nearer to an end. They were not torn down from the walls of Paris or Toulon; they were not brought from Minorca, in return for those which we lately lost. They came from a place so obscure and inconsiderable, that its name is known only to the French and English; and are purchased at an expence, which would be barely countervailed by the conquest of a province on the Continent, or the defeat of a royal army.

Surely our understandings are treated with too much contempt, when these fallacies are practised upon us; when we are entertained with such despicable processions, as equivalent to the expence of millions, and the death of thousands.

Let us no more boast, till something is performed; let us not exalt our enemies by telling mankind how highly we rate this petty conquest, and by confessing how much the slightest advantage has exceeded our hope.

September 30

To the Author of the *Universal Chronicle.*
Sir,
It was often said by the Earl of Oxford, that *a knot of idle fellows*

Observations (August–September 1758)

made a noise in one another's ears at a coffee-house, and imagined the nation to be filled with the same clamour. This seems to have been lately the case of the English Rabble; they have drank to the conquest of Louisbourg, till they take Louisbourg to be the seat of the Empire, and believe the rest of the world to be of the same opinion. When any of them are told, that the name of Louisbourg is not known but to the nations to whom a local and accidental interest make it important, they stare, and gape, and wonder, and drink again, and talk what neither themselves nor their hearers can understand, of *premises and conclusions, inexcusable ignorance, certain falsehood, spirit and complexion.*

The madness of a nation, at least of the English, seldom lasts long; a week is commonly sufficient to restore them to their senses. They begin already to be ashamed of the acclamations with which the French colours were attended; and, perhaps he that with so much vehemence, attacked my honest Observations, has, before this time, recovered from his delirious elevation of heart, and begins to wonder, what himself meant, when he called the capture of a poor fortress, a *decisive victory,* and the display of a few Colours, an *undoubted proof of the inferiority of France.*

These Colours, he confesses not to be torn down from Paris or Toulon, *but they were taken,* he says, *at a place, the possession of which is of ten times more importance to Great Britain, and an ample recompence for the loss of Minorca.* This was suitable to the madness of the first hour, when the news was brought of our conquest. But the people are now sober again, and nothing but strong drink will ever persuade them to believe, that Louisbourg and Paris are to be named together. The writer himself seems to have soared above the strength of his own credulity, and comes down from his height with very dangerous precipitation. *Louisbourg is of ten times more importance than Paris, and an ample recompence for the loss of Minorca.* The latter part of this sentence affirms very little in comparison with the former; and yet, I am afraid, it affirms more than is true. I shall not stay to compare the two places. At Minorca the disgrace was to us greater than the loss; we were overcome in the sight of every nation whose respect is to be desired: At Louisbourg the loss is to the French greater than the disgrace, for our victory has happened in a remote part of the world, at a place which nothing but this contest could make known,

Observations (August–September 1758)

and for which, when the enquirer has found it in the map, he wonders what can tempt us to dispute.

My censurer has proceeded to prove the importance of the acquisition, by informing us, *that the whole continent of North America now lies open to our army.*—Surely not all the wide continent. Ticonderoga must at least be excepted. I do not indeed see, how the state of the continent is much changed, by the capture of an island: I hope this zealous writer knows, that Cape Breton is only an island. The coasts of America are more open, but the continent is as it was before, nor have we yet made any further progress since Louisbourg was taken.

The real value of this conquest I have, in a former remark, endeavoured to shew. It is a loss to the French, but no great gain to the English. The expedition has been honourable and useful; but for the *wisdom and spirit required in the plan, or the resolution and integrity in the execution,* we must have another night of madness before they will be found. Narrow minds are always engrossed by the present scene. Where is the wisdom of knowing, that we are to take those fortresses of the enemy that annoy us, particularly that fortress which was taken in the last war? What integrity can be exerted in the capture of a castle, or what resolution has been shewn above the courage required in all the ordinary operations of war?

Let us do ourselves justice, and no more than justice; we had no need, and made no use of the resolution shewn by the French in the attack of Minorca.

It is the fate of great and of brave men to be made ridiculous, by idle processions, and ignorant panegyrists. I am pleased, like others, with every prosperous event; as having, like others, my interest involved in that of the nation. I was the first who congratulated my countrymen on our success at Cherburg; but I did not magnify it to another Dunkirk. I praise when I can praise with truth; and hope, that there will never again be need of swelling trifles into dignity, or of covering deficiency with splendid falshood.

I am, Sir,
Your humble servant.

5
The False Alarm
(1770)

One of the chief advantages derived by the present generation from the improvement and diffusion of Philosophy, is deliverance from unnecessary terrours, and exemption from false alarms. The unusual appearances, whether regular or accidental, which once spread consternation over ages of ignorance, are now the recreations of inquisitive security. The sun is no more lamented when it is eclipsed, than when it sets; and meteors play their coruscations without prognostick or prediction.

The advancement of political knowledge may be expected to produce in time the like effects. Causeless discontent and seditious violence will grow less frequent, and less formidable, as the science of Government is better ascertained by a diligent study of the theory of Man.

It is not indeed to be expected, that physical and political truth should meet with equal acceptance, or gain ground upon the world with equal facility. The notions of the naturalist find mankind in a state of neutrality, or at worst have nothing to encounter but prejudice and vanity; prejudice without malignity, and vanity without interest. But the politician's improvements are opposed by every passion that can exclude conviction or suppress it; by ambition, by avarice, by hope, and by terrour, by public faction, and private animosity.

It is evident, whatever be the cause, that this nation, with all its renown for speculation and for learning, has yet made little proficiency in civil wisdom. We are still so much unacquainted with our own state, and so unskilful in the pursuit of happiness, that we shudder without danger, complain without grievances, and suffer our quiet to be disturbed, and our commerce to be

The False Alarm

interrupted, by an opposition to the government, raised only by interest, and supported only by clamour, which yet has so far prevailed upon ignorance and timidity, that many favour it as reasonable, and many dread it as powerful.

What is urged by those who have been so industrious to spread suspicion, and incite fury from one end of the kingdom to the other, may be known by perusing the papers which have been at once presented as petitions to the King, and exhibited in print as remonstrances to the people. It may therefore not be improper to lay before the Public the reflections of a man who cannot favour the opposition, for he thinks it wicked, and cannot fear it, for he thinks it weak.

The grievance which has produced all this tempest of outrage, the oppression in which all other oppressions are included, the invasion which has left us no property, the alarm that suffers no patriot to sleep in quiet, is comprised in a vote of the House of Commons, by which the freeholders of Middlesex are deprived of a Briton's birth-right, representation in parliament.

They have indeed received the usual writ of election, but that writ, alas! was malicious mockery; they were insulted with the form, but denied the reality, for there was one man excepted from their choice.

Non de vi, neque cæde, nec veneno,
Sed lis est mihi de tribus capellis.

The character of the man thus fatally excepted, I have no purpose to delineate. Lampoon itself would disdain to speak ill of him of whom no man speaks well. It is sufficient that he is expelled the House of Commons, and confined in jail as being legally convicted of sedition and impiety.

That this man cannot be appointed one of the guardians and counsellors of the church and state, is a grievance not to be endured. Every lover of liberty stands doubtful of the fate of posterity, because the chief county in England cannot take its representative from a jail.

Whence Middlesex should obtain the right of being denominated the chief county, cannot easily be discovered; it is indeed the county where the chief city happens to stand, but how that city treated the favourite of Middlesex, is not yet forgotten. The county, as distinguished from the city, has no claim to particular consideration.

That a man was in jail for sedition and impiety, would, I believe, have been within memory a sufficient reason why he should not come out of jail a legislator. This reason, notwithstanding the mutability of fashion, happens still to operate on the House of Commons. Their notions, however strange, may be justified by a common observation, that few are mended by imprisonment, and that he whose crimes have made confinement necessary, seldom makes any other use of his enlargement, than to do with greater cunning what he did before with less.

But the people have been told with great confidence, that the House cannot control the right of constituting representatives; that he who can persuade lawful electors to chuse him, whatever be his character, is lawfully chosen, and has a claim to a seat in Parliament, from which no human authority can depose him.

Here, however, the patrons of opposition are in some perplexity. They are forced to confess, that by a train of precedents sufficient to establish a custom of Parliament, the House of Commons has jurisdiction over its own members; that the whole has power over individuals; and that this power has been exercised sometimes in imprisonment, and often in expulsion.

That such power should reside in the House of Commons in some cases, is inevitably necessary, since it is required by every polity, that where there is a possibility of offence, there should be a possibility of punishment. A member of the House cannot be cited for his conduct in Parliament before any other court; and therefore, if the House cannot punish him, he may attack with impunity the rights of the people, and the title of the King.

This exemption from the authority of other courts was, I think, first established in favour of the five members in the long parliament. It is not to be considered as an usurpation, for it is implied in the principles of government. If legislative powers are not coordinate, they cease in part to be legislative; and if they be coordinate, they are unaccountable; for to whom must that power account, which has no superiour?

The House of Commons is indeed dissoluble by the King, as the nation has of late been very clamorously told; but while it subsists it is co-ordinate with the other powers, and this co-ordination ceases only when the House by dissolution ceases to subsist.

As the particular representatives of the people are in their public character above the control of the courts of law, they must be subject to the jurisdiction of the House, and as the House, in the exercise of its authority, can be neither directed nor restrained, its own resolutions must be its laws, at least, if there is no antecedent decision of the whole legislature.

This privilege, not confirmed by any written law or positive compact, but by the resistless power of political necessity, they have exercised, probably from their first institution, but certainly, as their records inform us, from the 23d of Elizabeth, when they expelled a member for derogating from their privileges.

It may perhaps be doubted, whether it was originally necessary, that this right of control and punishment, should extend beyond offences in the exercise of parliamentary duty, since all other crimes are cognizable by other courts. But they, who are the only judges of their own rights, have exerted the power of expulsion on other occasions, and when wickedness arrived at a certain magnitude, have considered an offence against society as an offence against the House.

They have therefore divested notorious delinquents of their legislative character, and delivered them up to shame or punishment, naked and unprotected, that they might not contaminate the dignity of Parliament.

It is allowed that a man attainted of felony cannot sit in Parliament, and the Commons probably judged, that not being bound to the forms of law, they might treat these as felons, whose crimes were in their opinion equivalent to felony; and that as a known felon could not be chosen, a man so like a felon, that he could not easily be distinguished, ought to be expelled.

The first laws had no law to enforce them, the first authority was constituted by itself. The power exercised by the House of Commons is of this kind, a power rooted in the principles of government, and branched out by occasional practice; a power which necessity made just, and precedents have made legal.

It will occur that authority thus uncontrolable may, in times of heat and contest, be oppressively and injuriously exerted, and that

The False Alarm

he who suffers injustice, is without redress, however innocent, however miserable.

The position is true but the argument is useless. The Commons must be controlled, or be exempt from control. If they are exempt they may do injury which cannot be redressed, if they are controlled they are no longer legislative.

If the possibility of abuse be an argument against authority, no authority ever can be established; if the actual abuse destroys its legality, there is no legal government now in the world.

This power, which the Commons have so long exercised, they ventured to use once more against Mr. Wilkes, and on the 3d of February, 1769, expelled him the House, *for having printed and published a seditious libel, and three obscene and impious libels.*

If these imputations were just, the expulsion was surely seasonable, and that they were just, the House had reason to determine, as he had confessed himself, at the bar, the author of the libel which they term seditious, and was convicted in the King's Bench of both the publications.

But the Freeholders of Middlesex were of another opinion. They either thought him innocent, or were not offended by his guilt. When a writ was issued for the election of a knight for Middlesex, in the room of John Wilkes, Esq; expelled the House, his friends on the sixteenth of February chose him again.

On the 17th, it was resolved, *that* John Wilkes, Esq; *having been in this Session of Parliament expelled the House, was, and is, incapable of being elected a member to serve in this present Parliament.*

As there was no other candidate, it was resolved, at the same time, that the election of the sixteenth was a void election.

The Freeholders still continued to think that no other man was fit to represent them, and on the sixteenth of March elected him once more. Their resolution was now so well known, that no opponent ventured to appear.

The Commons began to find, that power without materials for operation can produce no effect. They might make the election void for ever, but if no other candidate could be found, their determination could only be negative. They, however, made void the last election, and ordered a new writ.

On the thirteenth of April was a new election, at which Mr.

The False Alarm

Lutterel, and others, offered themselves candidates. Every method of intimidation was used, and some acts of violence were done to hinder Mr. Lutterel from appearing. He was not deterred, and the poll was taken, which exhibited for Mr. Wilkes, — — 1143
Mr. Lutterel, — — 296
The sheriff returned Mr. Wilkes, but the House, on April the fifteenth, determined that Mr. Lutterel was lawfully elected.

From this day begun the clamour, which has continued till now. Those who had undertaken to oppose the ministry, having no grievance of greater magnitude, endeavoured to swell this decision into bulk, and distort it into deformity, and then held it out to terrify the nation.

Every artifice of sedition has been since practised to awaken discontent and inflame indignation. The papers of every day have been filled with the exhortations and menaces of faction. The madness has spread through all ranks and through both sexes; women and children have clamoured for Mr. Wilkes, honest simplicity has been cheated into fury, and only the wise have escaped infection.

The greater part may justly be suspected of not believing their own position, and with them it is not necessary to dispute. They cannot be convinced, who are convinced already, and it is well known that they will not be ashamed.

The decision, however, by which the smaller number of votes was preferred to the greater, has perplexed the minds of some, whose opinions it were indecent to despise, and who by their integrity well deserve to have their doubts appeased.

Every diffuse and complicated question may be examined by different methods, upon different principles; and that truth, which is easily found by one investigator, may be missed by another, equally honest and equally diligent.

Those who inquire, whether a smaller number of legal votes can elect a representative in opposition to a greater, must receive from every tongue the same answer.

The question, therefore, must be, whether a smaller number of legal votes, shall not prevail against a greater number of votes not legal.

It must be considered, that those votes only are legal which are legally given, and that those only are legally given, which are given for a legal candidate.

The False Alarm

It remains then to be discussed, whether a man expelled, can be so disqualified by a vote of the House, as that he shall be no longer eligible by lawful electors.

Here we must again recur, not to positive institutions, but to the unwritten law of social nature, to the great and pregnant principle of political necessity. All government supposes subjects, all authority implies obedience. To suppose in one the right to command what another has the right to refuse is absurd and contradictory. A state so constituted must rest for ever in motionless equipoise, with equal attractions of contrary tendency, with equal weights of power balancing each other.

Laws which cannot be enforced, can neither prevent nor rectify disorders. A sentence which cannot be executed can have no power to warn or to reform. If the Commons have only the power of dismissing for a few days the man whom his constituents can immediately send back, if they can expel but cannot exclude, they have nothing more than nominal authority, to which perhaps obedience never may be paid.

The representatives of our ancestors had an opinion very different: they fined and imprisoned their members; on great provocation they disabled them for ever, and this power of pronouncing perpetual disability is maintained by Selden himself.

These claims seem to have been made and allowed, when the constitution of our government had not yet been sufficiently studied. Such powers are not legal, because they are not necessary; and of that power which only necessity justifies, no more is to be admitted than necessity obtrudes.

The Commons cannot make laws, they can only pass resolutions, which, like all resolutions, are of force only to those that make them, and to those only while they are willing to observe them.

The vote of the House of Commons has therefore only so far the force of a law, as that force is necessary to preserve the vote from losing its efficacy, it must begin by operating upon themselves, and extends its influence to others, only by consequences arising from the first intention. He that starts game on his own manor, may pursue it into another.

They can properly make laws only for themselves: a member, while he keeps his seat, is subject to these laws; but when he is expelled, the jurisdiction ceases, for he is now no longer within their dominion.

The disability, which a vote can superinduce to expulsion, is no more than was included in expulsion itself; it is only a declaration of the Commons, that they will permit no longer him whom they thus censure to sit with them in Parliament; a declaration made by that right which they necessarily possess, of regulating their own House, and of inflicting punishment on their own delinquents.

They have therefore no other way to enforce the sentence of incapacity, than that of adhering to it. They cannot otherwise punish the candidate so disqualified for offering himself, nor the electors for accepting him. But if he has any competitor, that competitor must prevail, and if he has none, his election will be void; for the right of the House to reject, annihilates with regard to the man so rejected the right of electing.

It has been urged, that the power of the House terminates with their session; since a prisoner committed by the Speaker's warrant cannot be detained during the recess. That power indeed ceases with the session, which must operate by the agency of others, because, when they do not sit, they can employ no agent, having no longer any legal existence; but that which is exercised on themselves revives at their meeting, when the subject of that power still subsists. They can in the next session refuse to re-admit him, whom in the former session they expelled.

That expulsion inferred exclusion, in the present case, must be, I think, easily admitted. The expulsion and the writ issued for a new election were in the same session, and since the House is by the rule of Parliament bound for the session by a vote once passed, the expelled member cannot be admitted. He that cannot be admitted, cannot be elected, and the votes given to a man ineligible being given in vain, the highest number for an eligible candidate becomes a majority.

To these conclusions, as to most moral, and to all political positions, many objections may be made. The perpetual subject of political disquisition is not absolute, but comparative good. Of two systems of government, or two laws relating to the same subject, neither will ever be such as theoretical nicety would desire, and therefore neither can easily force its way against pre-

The False Alarm

judice and obstinacy; each will have its excellencies and defects, and every man, with a little help from pride, may think his own the best.

It seems to be the opinion of many, that expulsion is only a dismission of the representative to his constituents, with such a testimony against him as his sentence may comprise; and that if his constituents, notwithstanding the censure of the House, thinking his case hard, his fault trifling, or his excellencies such as overbalance it, should again chuse him as still worthy of their trust, the House cannot refuse him, for his punishment has purged his fault, and the right of electors must not be violated.

This is plausible but not cogent. It is a scheme of representation, which would make a specious appearance in a political romance, but cannot be brought into practice among us, who see every day the towering head of speculation bow down unwillingly to groveling experience.

Governments formed by chance, and gradually improved by such expedients, as the successive discovery of their defects happened to suggest, are never to be tried by a regular theory. They are fabricks of dissimilar materials, raised by different architects, upon different plans. We must be content with them as they are; should we attempt to mend their disproportions, we might easily demolish, and difficultly rebuild them.

Laws are now made, and customs are established; these are our rules, and by them we must be guided.

It is uncontrovertibly certain, that the Commons never intended to leave electors the liberty of returning them an expelled member, for they always require one to be chosen in the room of him that is expelled, and I see not with what propriety a man can be rechosen in his own room.

Expulsion, if this were its whole effect, might very often be desirable. Sedition, or obscenity, might be no greater crimes in the opinion of other electors, than in that of the freeholders of Middlesex; and many a wretch, whom his colleagues should expel, might come back persecuted into fame, and provoke with harder front a second expulsion.

Many of the representatives of the people can hardly be said to have been chosen at all. Some by inheriting a borough inherit a seat; and some sit by the favour of others, whom perhaps they may gratify by the act which provoked the expulsion. Some are safe by their popularity, and some by their alliances. None would dread expulsion, if this doctrine were received, but those who bought their elections, and who would be obliged to buy them again at a higher price.

But as uncertainties are to be determined by things certain, and customs to be explained, where it is possible, by written law, the patriots have triumphed with a quotation from an act of the *4th* and *5th* of *Anne*, which permits those to be rechosen, whose seats are vacated by the acceptance of a place of profit. This they wisely consider as an expulsion, and from the permission, in this case, of a re-election, infer that every other expulsion leaves the delinquent entitled to the same indulgence. This is the paragraph.

> If any person, *being chosen a member* of the House of Commons, shall accept of any office from the crown, *during such time as he shall continue a member*, his election shall be, and is hereby declared to be void, and a new writ shall issue for a new election, as if such person so accepting was naturally dead. *Nevertheless such person shall be capable of being again elected*, as if his place had not become void as aforesaid.

How this favours the doctrine of re-admission by a second choice, I am not able to discover. The statute of 30 Ch. II. had enacted, That *he who should sit in the House of Commons, without taking the oaths and subscribing the test, should be disabled to sit in the House during that Parliament, and a writ should issue for the election of a new member, in place of the member so disabled, as if such member had naturally died.*

This last clause is apparently copied in the act of Anne, but with the common fate of imitators. In the act of Charles, the political death continued during the Parliament, in that of Anne it was hardly worth the while to kill the man whom the next breath was to revive. It is, however, apparent, that in the opinion of the Parliament, the dead-doing lines would have kept him motionless, if he had not been recovered by a kind exception. A seat vacated, could not be regained without express permission of the same statute.

The right of being chosen again to a seat thus vacated, is not enjoyed by any general right, but required a special clause, and solicitous provision.

The False Alarm

But what resemblance can imagination conceive between one man vacating his seat, by a mark of favour from the crown, and another driven from it for sedition and obscenity. The acceptance of a place contaminates no character; the crown that gives it, intends to give with it always dignity, sometimes authority. The Commons, it is well known, think not worse of themselves or others for their offices of profit; yet profit implies temptation, and may expose a representative to the suspicion of his constituents; though if they still think him worthy of their confidence, they may again elect him.

Such is the consequence. When a man is dismissed by law to his constituents, with new trust and new dignity, they may, if they think him incorruptible, restore him to his seat; what can follow, therefore, but that when the House drives out a varlet with public infamy, he goes away with the like permission to return.

If infatuation be, as the proverb tells us, the forerunner of destruction, how near must be the ruin of a nation that can be incited against it's governors, by sophistry like this. I may be excused if I catch the panick, and join my groans at this alarming crisis, with the general lamentation of weeping patriots.

Another objection is, that the Commons, by pronouncing the sentence of disqualification, make a law, and take upon themselves the power of the whole legislature. Many quotations are then produced to prove that the House of Commons can make no laws.

Three acts have been cited, disabling members for different terms on different occasions, and it is profoundly remarked, that if the Commons could by their own privilege have made a disqualification, their jealousy of their privileges would never have admitted the concurrent sanction of the other powers.

I must for ever remind these puny controvertists, that those acts are laws of permanent obligation: that two of them are now in force, and that the other expired only when it had fulfilled its end. Such laws the Commons cannot make; they could, perhaps, have determined for themselves, that they would expel all who should not take the test, but they could leave no authority behind them, that should oblige the next Parliament to expel them. They could refuse the South Sea directors, but they could not entail the refusal. They can disqualify by vote, but not by law; they cannot know that the sentence of disqualification pronounced to-day may not become void to-morrow, by the dissolution of their own House. Yet while the same Parliament sits, the disqualification continues unless the vote be rescinded, and while it so continues, makes the votes, which freeholders may give to the interdicted candidate, useless and dead, since there cannot exist, with respect to the same subject at the same time, an absolute power to chuse and an absolute power to reject.

In 1614, the attorney-general was voted incapable of a seat in the House of Commons, and the nation is triumphantly told, that though the vote never was revoked, the attorney-general is now a member. He certainly may now be a member without revocation of the vote. A law is of perpetual obligation, but a vote is nothing when the voters are gone. A law is a compact reciprocally made by the legislative powers, and therefore not to be abrogated but by all the parties. A vote is simply a resolution, which binds only him that is willing to be bound.

I have thus punctiliously and minutely persued this disquisition, because I suspect that these reasoners, whose business is to deceive others, have sometimes deceived themselves, and I am willing to free them from their embarrassment, though I do not expect much gratitude for my kindness.

Other objections are yet remaining, for of political objections there cannot easily be an end. It has been observed, that vice is no proper cause of expulsion, for if the worst man in the House were always to be expelled, in time none would be left. But no man is expelled for being worst, he is expelled for being enormously bad; his conduct is compared, not with that of others, but with the rule of action.

The punishment of expulsion being in its own nature uncertain, may be too great or too little for the fault.

This must be the case of many punishments. Forfeiture of chattels is nothing to him that has no possessions. Exile itself may be accidentally a good; and indeed any punishment less than death is very different to different men.

But if this precedent be admitted and established, no man can hereafter be sure that he shall be represented by him whom he would choose. One half of the House may meet early in the morning, and snatch an opportunity to expel the other, and the

The False Alarm

greater part of the nation may by this stratagem be without its lawful representatives.

He that sees all this, sees very far. But I can tell him of greater evils yet behind. There is one possibility of wickedness, which, at this alarming crisis, has not yet been mentioned. Every one knows the malice, the subtilty, the industry, the vigilance, and the greediness of the Scots. The Scotch members are about the number sufficient to make a house. I propose it to the consideration of the Supporters of the Bill of Rights, whether there is not reason to suspect, that these hungry intruders from the North, are now contriving to expel all the English. We may then curse the hour in which it was determined, that expulsion and exclusion are the same. For who can guess what may be done when the Scots have the whole House to themselves?

Thus agreeable to custom and reason, notwithstanding all objections, real or imaginary, thus consistent with the practice of former times, and thus consequential to the original principles of government, is that decision by which so much violence of discontent has been excited, which has been so dolorously bewailed, and so outrageously resented.

Let us however not be seduced to put too much confidence in justice or in truth, they have often been found inactive in their own defence, and give more confidence than help to their friends and their advocates. It may perhaps be prudent to make one momentary concession to falsehood, by supposing the vote in Mr. Lutterel's favour to be wrong.

All wrong ought to be rectified. If Mr. Wilkes is deprived of a lawful seat, both he and his electors have reason to complain; but it will not be easily found, why, among the innumerable wrongs of which a great part of mankind are hourly complaining, the whole care of the Public should be transferred to Mr. Wilkes and the freeholders of Middlesex, who might all sink into non-existence, without any other effect, than that there would be room made for a new rabble, and a new retailer of sedition and obscenity. The cause of our country would suffer little; the rabble, whencesoever they come, will be always patriots, and always Supporters of the Bill of Rights.

The House of Commons decides the disputes arising from elections. Was it ever supposed, that in all cases their decisions were right? Every man whose lawful election is defeated, is equally wronged with Mr. Wilkes, and his constituents feel their disappointment with no less anguish than the freeholders of Middlesex. These decisions have often been apparently partial, and sometimes tyrannically oppressive. A majority has been given to a favourite candidate, by expunging votes which had always been allowed, and which therefore had the authority by which all votes are given, that of custom uninterrupted. When the Commons determine who shall be constituents, they may, with some propriety, be said to make law, because those determinations have hitherto, for the sake of quiet, been adopted by succeeding Parliaments. A vote therefore of the House, when it operates as a law, is to individuals a law only temporary, but to communities perpetual.

Yet though all this has been done, and though at every new Parliament much of this is expected to be done again, it has never produced in any former time such an *alarming crisis*. We have found by experience, that though a squire has given ale and venison in vain, and a borough has been compelled to see its dearest interest in the hands of him whom it did not trust, yet the general state of the nation has continued the same. The sun has risen, and the corn has grown, and whatever talk has been of the danger of property, yet he that ploughed the field commonly reaped it, and he that built a house was master of the door: the vexation excited by injustice suffered, or supposed to be suffered, by any private man, or single community, was local and temporary, it neither spread far, nor lasted long.

The nation looked on with little care, because there did not seem to be much danger. The consequence of small irregularities was not felt, and we had not yet learned to be terrified by very distant enemies.

But quiet and security are now at an end. Our vigilance is quickened, and our comprehension is enlarged. We not only see events in their causes, but before their causes; we hear the thunder while the sky is clear, and see the mine sprung before it is dug. Political wisdom has, by the force of English genius, been improved at last not only to political intuition, but to political prescience.

But it cannot, I am afraid, be said, that as we are grown wise,

The False Alarm

we are made happy. It is said of those who have the wonderful power called second sight, that they seldom see any thing but evil: political second sight has the same effect; we hear of nothing but of an alarming crisis, of violated rights, and expiring liberties. The morning rises upon new wrongs, and the dreamer passes the night in imaginary shackles.

The sphere of anxiety is now enlarged; he that hitherto cared only for himself, now cares for the Public; for he has learned that the happiness of individuals is comprised in the prosperity of the whole, and that his country never suffers but he suffers with it, however it happens that he feels no pain.

Fired with this fever of epidemic patriotism, the taylor slips his thimble, the drapier drops his yard, and the blacksmith lays down his hammer; they meet at an honest alehouse, consider the state of the nation, read or hear the last petition, lament the miseries of the time, are alarmed at the dreadful crisis, and subscribe to the support of the Bill of Rights.

It sometimes indeed happens, that an intruder of more benevolence than prudence attempts to disperse their cloud of dejection, and ease their hearts by seasonable consolation. He tells them, that though the government cannot be too diligently watched, it may be too hastily accused; and that, though private judgment is every man's right, yet we cannot judge of what we do not know; that we feel at present no evils which government can alleviate, and that the public business is committed to men who have as much right to confidence as their adversaries; that the freeholders of Middlesex, if they could not choose Mr. Wilkes, might have chosen any other man, and that *he trusts we have within the realm five hundred as good as he:* that even if this which has happened to Middlesex had happened to every other county, that one man should be made incapable of being elected, it could produce no great change in the Parliament, nor much contract the power of election; that what has been done is probably right, and that if it be wrong it is of little consequence, since a like case cannot easily occur; that expulsions are very rare, and if they should, by unbounded insolence of faction, become more frequent, the electors may easily provide a second choice.

All this he may say, but not half of this will be heard; his opponents will stun him and themselves with a confused sound of pension and places, venality and corruption, oppression and invasion, slavery and ruin.

Outcries like these, uttered by malignity, and ecchoed by folly; general accusations of indeterminate wickedness; and obscure hints of impossible designs, dispersed among those that do not know their meaning, by those that know them to be false, have disposed part of the nation, though but a small part, to pester the court with ridiculous petitions.

The progress of a petition is well known. An ejected placeman goes down to his county or his borough, tells his friends of his inability to serve them, and his constituents of the corruption of the government. His friends readily understand that he who can get nothing, will have nothing to give. They agree to proclaim a meeting; meat and drink are plentifully provided; a crowd is easily brought together, and those who think that they know the reason of their meeting, undertake to tell those who know it not. Ale and clamour unite their powers, the crowd, condensed and heated, begins to ferment with the leven of sedition. All see a thousand evils though they cannot show them, and grow impatient for a remedy, though they know not what.

A speech is then made by the Cicero of the day, he says much, and suppresses more, and credit is equally given to what he tells, and what he conceals. The petition is read and universally approved. Those who are sober enough to write, add their names, and the rest would sign it if they could.

Every man goes home and tells his neighbour of the glories of the day; how he was consulted and what he advised; how he was invited into the great room, where his lordship called him by his name; how he was caressed by Sir Francis, Sir Joseph, or Sir George; how he eat turtle and venison, and drank unanimity to the three brothers.

The poor loiterer, whose shop had confined him, or whose wife had locked him up, hears the tale of luxury with envy, and at last inquires what was their petition. Of the petition nothing is remembered by the narrator, but that it spoke much of fears and apprehensions, and something very alarming, and that he is sure it is against the government; the other is convinced that it must be right, and wishes he had been there, for he loves wine and venison, and is resolved as long as he lives to be against the government.

The False Alarm

The petition is then handed from town to town, and from house to house, and wherever it comes the inhabitants flock together, that they may see that which must be sent to the King. Names are easily collected. One man signs because he hates the papists; another because he has vowed destruction to the turnpikes; one because it will vex the parson; another because he owes his landlord nothing; one because he is rich; another because he is poor; one to shew that he is not afraid, and another to shew that he can write.

The passage, however, is not always smooth. Those who collect contributions to sedition, sometimes apply to a man of higher rank and more enlightened mind, who instead of lending them his name, calmly reproves them for being seducers of the people.

You who are here, says he, complaining of venality, are yourselves the agents of those, who having estimated themselves at too high a price, are only angry that they are not bought. You are appealing from the parliament to the rabble, and inviting those, who scarcely, in the most common affairs, distinguish right from wrong, to judge of a question complicated with law written and unwritten, with the general principles of government, and the particular customs of the House of Commons; you are shewing them a grievance, so distant that they cannot see it, and so light that they cannot feel it; for how, but by unnecessary intelligence and artificial provocation, should the farmers and shopkeepers of Yorkshire and Cumberland know or care how Middlesex is represented. Instead of wandering thus round the county to exasperate the rage of party, and darken the suspicions of ignorance, it is the duty of men like you, who have leisure for inquiry, to lead back the people to their honest labour; to tell them, that submission is the duty of the ignorant, and content the virtue of the poor; that they have no skill in the art of government, nor any interest in the dissensions of the great; and when you meet with any, as some there are, whose understandings are capable of conviction, it will become you to allay this foaming ebullition, by shewing them that they have as much happiness as the condition of life will easily receive, and that a government, of which an erroneous or unjust representation of Middlesex is the greatest crime that interest can discover, or malice can upbraid, is a government approaching nearer to perfection, than any that experience has known, or history related.

The False Alarm

The drudges of sedition wish to change their ground, they hear him with sullen silence, feel conviction without repentance, and are confounded but not abashed; they go forward to another door, and find a kinder reception from a man enraged against the government, because he has just been paying the tax upon his windows.

That a petition for a dissolution of the Parliament will at all time have its favourers, may be easily imagined. The people indeed do not expect that one House of Commons will be much honester or much wiser than another; they do not suppose that the taxes will be lightened; or though they have been so often taught to hope it, that soap and candles will be cheaper; they expect no redress of grievances, for of no grievances but taxes do they complain; they wish not the extension of liberty, for they do not feel any restraint; about the security of privilege or property they are totally careless, for they see no property invaded, nor know, till they are told, that any privilege has suffered violation.

Least of all do they expect, that any future Parliament will lessen its own powers, or communicate to the people that authority which it has once obtained.

Yet a new Parliament is sufficiently desirable. The year of election is a year of jollity; and what is still more delightful, a year of equality. The glutton now eats the delicacies for which he longed when he could not purchase them, and the drunkard has the pleasure of wine without the cost. The drone lives a-while without work, and the shopkeeper, in the flow of money, raises his price. The mechanic that trembled at the presence of Sir Joseph, now bids him come again for an answer; and the poacher whose gun has been seized, now finds an opportunity to reclaim it. Even the honest man is not displeased to see himself important, and willingly resumes in two years that power which he had resigned for seven. Few love their friends so well as not to desire superiority by unexpensive benefaction.

Yet, notwithstanding all these motives to compliance, the promoters of petitions have not been successful. Few could be persuaded to lament evils which they did not suffer, or to solicit for redress which they do not want. The petition has been, in some places, rejected; and perhaps in all but one, signed only by the meanest and grossest of the people.

The False Alarm

Since this expedient now invented or revived to distress the government, and equally practicable at all times by all who shall be excluded from power and from profit, has produced so little effect, let us consider the opposition as no longer formidable. The great engine has recoiled upon them. They thought that *the terms* they *sent were terms of weight*, which would have *amazed all and stumbled many*; but the consternation is now over, and their foes *stand upright*, as before.

With great propriety and dignity the king has, in his speech, neglected or forgotten them. He might easily know, that what was presented as the sense of the people, is the sense only of the profligate and dissolute; and that whatever Parliament should be convened, the same petitions would be ready, for the same reason, to request its dissolution.

As we once had a rebellion of the clowns, we have now an opposition of the pedlars. The quiet of the nation has been for years disturbed by a faction, against which all factions ought to conspire; for its original principle is the desire of levelling; it is only animated under the name of zeal, by the natural malignity of the mean against the great.

When in the confusion which the English invasions produced in France, the villains, imagining that they had found the golden hour of emancipation, took arms in their hands, the knights of both nations considered the cause as common, and, suspending the general hostility, united to chastise them.

The whole conduct of this despicable faction is distinguished by plebeian grossness, and savage indecency. To misrepresent the actions and the principles of their enemies is common to all parties; but the insolence of invective, and brutality of reproach, which have lately prevailed, are peculiar to this.

An infallible characteristic of meanness is cruelty. This is the only faction that has shouted at the condemnation of a criminal, and that, when his innocence procured his pardon, has clamoured for his blood.

All other parties, however enraged at each other, have agreed to treat the throne with decency; but these low-born railers have attacked not only the authority, but the character of their Sovereign, and have endeavoured, surely without effect, to alienate the affections of the people from the only king, who, for almost a century, has much appeared to desire, or much endeavoured to deserve them. They have insulted him with rudeness and with menaces, which were never excited by the gloomy sullenness of William, even when half the nation denied him their allegiance; nor by the dangerous bigotry of James, unless when he was finally driven from his palace; and with which scarcely the open hostilities of rebellion ventured to vilify the unhappy Charles, even in the remarks on the cabinet of Naseby.

It is surely not unreasonable to hope, that the nation will consult its dignity, if not its safety, and disdain to be protected or enslaved by the declaimers or the plotters of a city-tavern. Had Rome fallen by the Catilinarian conspiracy, she might have consoled her fate by the greatness of her destroyers; but what would have alleviated the disgrace of England, had her government been changed by Tiler or by Ket?

One part of the nation has never before contended with the other, but for some weighty and apparent interest. If the means were violent, the end was great. The civil war was fought for what each army called and believed the best religion, and the best government. The struggle in the reign of Anne, was to exclude or restore an exiled king. We are now disputing, with almost equal animosity, whether Middlesex shall be represented or not by a criminal from a jail.

The only comfort left in such degeneracy is, that a lower state can be no longer possible.

In this contemptuous censure, I mean not to include every single man. In all lead, says the chemist, there is silver; and in all copper there is gold. But mingled masses are justly denominated by the greater quantity, and when the precious particles are not worth extraction, a faction and a pig must be melted down together to the forms and offices that chance allots them.

Fiunt urceoli, pelves, sartago, patellæ.

A few weeks will now shew whether the Government can be shaken by empty noise, and whether the faction which depends upon its influence, has not deceived alike the Public and itself. That it should have continued till now, is sufficiently shameful. None can indeed wonder that it has been supported by the sectaries, the natural fomenters of sedition, and confederates of the rabble, of whose religion little now remains but hatred of establishments, and who are angry to find separation now only tolerated, which was once rewarded; but every honest man must lament, that it has been regarded with frigid neutrality by the Tories, who, being long accustomed to signalize their principles by opposition to the court, do not yet consider that they have at last a king who knows not the name of party, and who wishes to be the common father of all his people.

As a man inebriated only by vapours, soon recovers in the open air; a nation discontented to madness, without any adequate cause, will return to its wits and its allegiance when a little pause has cooled it to reflection. Nothing, therefore, is necessary, at this *alarming crisis*, but to consider the alarm as false. To make concessions is to encourage encroachment. Let the court despise the faction, and the disappointed people will soon deride it.

6

Thoughts on the Late Transactions respecting Falkland's Islands
(1771)

To proportion the eagerness of contest to its importance seems too hard a task for human wisdom. The pride of wit has kept ages busy in the discussion of useless questions, and the pride of power has destroyed armies to gain or to keep unprofitable possessions.

Not many years have passed since the cruelties of war were filling the world with terror and with sorrow; rage was at last appeased, or strength exhausted, and to the harrassed nations peace was restored, with its pleasures and its benefits. Of this state all felt the happiness, and all implored the continuance; but what continuance of happiness can be expected, when the whole system of European empire can be in danger of a new concussion, by a contention for a few spots of earth, which, in the deserts of the ocean, had almost escaped human notice, and which, if they had not happened to make a sea-mark, had perhaps never had a name.

Fortune often delights to dignify what nature has neglected, and that renown which cannot be claimed by intrinsick excellence or greatness, is sometimes derived from unexpected accidents. The Rubicon was ennobled by the passage of Cæsar, and the time is now come when Falkland's Islands demand their historian.

But the writer to whom this employment shall be assigned, will have few opportunities of descriptive splendor, or narrative elegance. Of other countries it is told how often they have changed their government; these islands have hitherto changed only their name. Of heroes to conquer, or legislators to civilize, here has been

Thoughts on the Late Transactions respecting Falkland's Islands

no appearance; nothing has happened to them but that they have been sometimes seen by wandering navigators, who passed by them in search of better habitations.

When the Spaniards, who, under the conduct of Columbus, discovered America, had taken possession of its most wealthy regions; they surprised and terrified Europe by a sudden and unexampled influx of riches. They were made at once insupportably insolent, and might perhaps have become irresistibly powerful, had not their mountainous treasures been scattered in the air with the ignorant profusion of unaccustomed opulence.

The greater part of the European potentates saw this stream of riches flowing into Spain without attempting to dip their own hands in the golden fountain. France had no naval skill or power; Portugal was extending her dominions in the East over regions formed in the gaiety of Nature; the Hanseatic league, being planned only for the security of traffick, had no tendency to discovery or invasion; and the commercial states of Italy growing rich by trading between Asia and Europe, and not lying upon the ocean, did not desire to seek by great hazards, at a distance, what was almost at home to be found with safety.

The English alone were animated by the success of the Spanish navigators, to try if any thing was left that might reward adventure, or incite appropriation. They sent Cabot into the North, but in the North there was no gold or silver to be found. The best regions were pre-occupied, yet they still continued their hopes and their labours. They were the second nation that dared the extent of the Pacifick Ocean, and the second circumnavigators of the globe.

By the war between Elizabeth and Philip, the wealth of America became lawful prize, and those who were less afraid of danger than of poverty, supposed that riches might easily be obtained by plundering the Spaniards. Nothing is difficult when gain and honour unite their influence; the spirit and vigour of these expeditions enlarged our views of the new world, and made us first acquainted with its remoter coasts.

In the fatal voyage of Cavendish (1592) Captain Davis, who, being sent out as his associate, was afterwards parted from him or deserted him, as he was driven by violence of weather about the Straits of Magellan, is supposed to have been the first who saw the lands now called Falkland's Islands, but his distress permitted

Thoughts on the Late Transactions respecting Falkland's Islands

him not to make any observation, and he left them, as he found them, without a name.

Not long afterwards (1594) Sir Richard Hawkins, being in the same seas with the same designs, saw these islands again, if they are indeed the same islands, and in honour of his mistress, called them Hawkins's Maiden Land.

This voyage was not of renown sufficient to procure a general reception to the new name, for when the Dutch, who had now become strong enough not only to defend themselves, but to attack their masters, sent (1598) Verhagen and Sebald de Wert, into the South Sea, these Islands, which were not supposed to have been known before, obtained the denomination of Sebald's Islands, and were from that time placed in the charts; though Frezier tells us, that they were yet considered as of doubtful existence.

Their present English name was probably given them (1689) by Strong, whose journal, yet unprinted, may be found in the Museum. This name was adopted by Halley, and has from that time, I believe, been received into our maps.

The privateers which were put into motion by the wars of William and Anne, saw those islands and mention them; but they were yet not considered as territories worth a contest. Strong affirmed that there was no wood, and Dampier suspected that they had no water.

Frezier describes their appearance with more distinctness, and mentions some ships of St. Maloes, by which they had been visited, and to which he seems willing enough to ascribe the honour of discovering islands which yet he admits to have been seen by Hawkins, and named by Sebald de Wert. He, I suppose, in honour of his countrymen, called them the Malouines, the denomination now used by the Spaniards, who seem not, till very lately, to have thought them important enough to deserve a name.

Since the publication of Anson's voyage, they have very much changed their opinion, finding a settlement in Pepys's or Falkland's Island recommended by the author as necessary to the success of our future expeditions against the coast of Chili, and as of such use and importance, that it would produce many advantages in peace, and in war would make us masters of the South Sea.

Thoughts on the Late Transactions respecting Falkland's Islands

Scarcely any degree of judgment is sufficient to restrain the imagination from magnifying that on which it is long detained. The relator of Anson's voyage had heated his mind with its various events, had partaken the hope with which it was begun, and the vexation suffered by its various miscarriages, and then thought nothing could be of greater benefit to the nation than that which might promote the success of such another enterprise.

Had the heroes of that history even performed and attained all that when they first spread their sails they ventured to hope, the consequence would yet have produced very little hurt to the Spaniards, and very little benefit to the English. They would have taken a few towns; Anson and his companions would have shared the plunder or the ransom; and the Spaniards, finding their southern territories accessible, would for the future have guarded them better.

That such a settlement may be of use in war, no man that considers its situation will deny. But war is not the whole business of life; it happens but seldom, and every man, either good or wise, wishes that its frequency were still less. That conduct which betrays designs of future hostility, if it does not excite violence, will always generate malignity; it must for ever exclude confidence and friendship, and continue a cold and sluggish rivalry, by a sly reciprocation of indirect injuries, without the bravery of war, or the security of peace.

The advantage of such a settlement in time of peace is, I think, not easily to be proved. For what use can it have but of a station for contraband traders, a nursery of fraud, and a receptacle of theft? Narborough, about a century ago, was of opinion, that no advantage could be obtained in voyages to the South Sea, except by such an armament as, with a sailor's morality, *might trade by force*. It is well known that the prohibitions of foreign commerce are, in these countries, to the last degree rigorous, and that no man not authorized by the King of Spain can trade there but by force or stealth. Whatever profit is obtained must be gained by the violence of rapine, or dexterity of fraud.

Government will not perhaps soon arrive at such purity and excellence, but that some connivance at least will be indulged to the triumphant robber and successful cheat. He that brings wealth home is seldom interrogated by what means it was obtained. This, however, is one of those modes of corruption with which mankind ought always to struggle, and which they may in time hope to overcome. There is reason to expect, that as the world is more enlightened, policy and morality will at last be reconciled, and that nations will learn not to do what they would not suffer.

But the silent toleration of suspected guilt is a degree of depravity far below that which openly incites and manifestly protects it. To pardon a pirate may be injurious to mankind; but how much greater is the crime of opening a port in which all pirates shall be safe? The contraband trader is not more worthy of protection: if with Narborough he trades by force, he is a pirate; if he trades secretly, he is only a thief. Those who honestly refuse his traffick he hates as obstructors of his profit; and those with whom he deals he cheats, because he knows that they dare not complain. He lives with a heart full of that malignity which fear of detection always generates in those who are to defend unjust acquisitions against lawful authority; and when he comes home with riches thus acquired, he brings a mind hardened in evil, too proud for reproof, and too stupid for reflection; he offends the high by his insolence, and corrupts the low by his example.

Whether these truths were forgotten or despised, or whether some better purpose was then in agitation, the representation made in Anson's voyage had such effect upon the statesmen of that time, that (in 1748) some sloops were fitted out for the fuller knowledge of Pepys and Falkland's Islands, and for further discoveries in the South Sea. This expedition, though perhaps designed to be secret, was not long concealed from *Wall*, the Spanish ambassador, who so vehemently opposed it, and so strongly maintained the right of the Spaniards to the exclusive dominion of the South Sea, that the English ministry relinquished part of their original design, and declared that the examination of those two Islands was the utmost that their orders should comprise.

This concession was sufficiently liberal or sufficiently submissive; yet the Spanish court was neither gratified by our kindness, nor softened by our humility. Sir Benjamin Keene, who then resided at Madrid, was interrogated by Carvajal concerning the visit intended to Pepys' and Falkland's Islands in terms of great jealousy and discontent; and the intended expedition was represented, if not as a direct violation of the late peace, yet as an act

Thoughts on the Late Transactions respecting Falkland's Islands

inconsistent with amicable intentions, and contrary to the professions of mutual kindness which then passed between Spain and England. Keene was directed to protest that nothing more than mere discovery was intended, and that no settlement was to be established. The Spaniard readily replied, that if this was a voyage of wanton curiosity, it might be gratified with less trouble, for he was willing to communicate whatever was known: That to go so far only to come back, was no reasonable act; and it would be a slender sacrifice to peace and friendship to omit a voyage in which nothing was to be gained: That if we left the places as we found them, the voyage was useless; and if we took possession, it was a hostile armament, nor could we expect that the Spaniards would suppose us to visit the southern parts of America only from curiosity, after the scheme proposed by the author of Anson's Voyage.

When once we had disowned all purpose of settling, it is apparent that we could not defend the propriety of our expedition by arguments equivalent to Carvajal's objections. The ministry therefore dismissed the whole design, but no declaration was required by which our right to persue it hereafter might be annulled.

From this time Falkland's Island was forgotten or neglected, till the conduct of naval affairs was intrusted to the Earl of Egmont, a man whose mind was vigorous and ardent, whose knowledge was extensive, and whose designs were magnificent; but who had somewhat vitiated his judgement by too much indulgence of romantick projects and airy speculations.

Lord Egmont's eagerness after something new determined him to make inquiry after Falkland's Island, and he sent out Captain Byron, who, in the beginning of the year 1765, took, he says, a formal possession in the name of his Britannick Majesty.

The possession of this place is, according to Mr. Byron's representation, no despicable acquisition. He conceived the island to be six or seven hundred miles round, and represented it as a region naked indeed of wood, but which, if that defect were supplied, would have all that nature, almost all that luxury could want. The harbour he found capacious and secure, and therefore thought it worthy of the name of Egmont. Of water there was no want, and the ground, he described as having all the excellencies of soil, and as covered with antiscorbutick herbs, the restoratives of the sailor. Provision was easily to be had, for they killed almost every day an hundred geese to each ship, by pelting them with stones. Not content with physick and with food, he searched yet deeper for the value of the new dominion. He dug in quest of ore, found iron in abundance, and did not despair of nobler metals.

A country thus fertile and delightful, fortunately found where none would have expected it, about the fiftieth degree of southern latitude, could not without great supineness be neglected. Early in the next year (January 8, 1766) Captain Macbride arrived at Port Egmont, where he erected a small blockhouse, and stationed a garrison. His description was less flattering. He found, what he calls, a mass of islands and broken lands, of which the soil was nothing but a bog, with no better prospect than that of barren mountains, beaten by storms almost perpetual. Yet this, says he, is summer, and if the winds of winter hold their natural proportion, those who lie but two cables length from the shore, must pass weeks without any communication with it. The plenty which regaled Mr. Byron, and which might have supported not only armies, but armies of Patagons, was no longer to be found. The geese were too wise to stay when men violated their haunts, and Mr. Macbride's crew could only now and then kill a goose when the weather would permit. All the quadrupeds which he met there were foxes, supposed by him to have been brought upon the ice; but of useless animals, such as sea lions and penguins, which he calls vermin, the number was incredible. He allows, however, that those who touch at these islands may find geese and snipes, and in the summer months, wild cellery and sorrel.

No token was seen by either, of any settlement ever made upon this island, and Mr. Macbride thought himself so secure from hostile disturbance, that when he erected his wooden blockhouse he omitted to open the ports and loopholes.

When a garrison was stationed at Port Egmont, it was necessary to try what sustenance the ground could be by culture excited to produce. A garden was prepared, but the plants that sprung up, withered away in immaturity. Some fir-seeds were sown; but though this be the native tree of rugged climates, the young firs that rose above the ground died like weaker herbage. The cold continued long, and the ocean seldom was at rest.

Thoughts on the Late Transactions respecting Falkland's Islands

Cattle succeeded better than vegetables. Goats, sheep, and hogs, that were carried thither, were found to thrive and increase as in other places.

Nil mortalibus arduum est. There is nothing which human courage will not undertake, and little that human patience will not endure. The garrison lived upon Falkland's Island, shrinking from the blast, and shuddering at the billows.

This was a colony which could never become independent, for it never could be able to maintain itself. The necessary supplies were annually sent from England, at an expence which the Admiralty began to think would not quickly be repaid. But shame of deserting a project, and unwillingness to contend with a projector that meant well, continued the garrison, and supplied it with regular remittances of stores and provision.

That of which we were almost weary ourselves, we did not expect any one to envy; and therefore supposed that we should be permitted to reside in Falkland's Island, the undisputed lords of tempest-beaten barrenness.

But, on the 28th of November 1769, Captain Hunt, observing a Spanish schooner hovering about the island and surveying it, sent the commander a message, by which he required him to depart. The Spaniard made an appearance of obeying, but in two days came back with letters written by the governor of Port Solidad, and brought by the chief officer of a settlement on the east part of Falkland's Island.

In this letter, dated *Malouina,* November 30, the governor complains, that Captain Hunt, when he ordered the schooner to depart, assumed a power to which he could have no pretensions, by sending an imperious message to the Spaniards in the King of Spain's own dominions.

In another letter sent at the same time, he supposes the English to be in that part only by accident, and to be ready to depart at the first warning. This letter was accompanied by a present, of which, says he, *if it be neither equal to my desire nor to your merit, you must impute the deficiency to the situation of us both.*

In return to this hostile civility, Captain Hunt warned them from the island, which he claimed in the name of the King, as belonging to the English by right of the first discovery and the first settlement.

Thoughts on the Late Transactions respecting Falkland's Islands

This was an assertion of more confidence than certainty. The right of discovery indeed has already appeared to be probable, but the right which priority of settlement confers I know not whether we yet can establish.

On December 10, the officer sent by the governor of Port Solidad made three protests against Captain Hunt; for threatening to fire upon him; for opposing his entrance into Port Egmont; and for entering himself into Port Solidad. On the 12th the governor of Port Solidad formally warned Captain Hunt to leave Port Egmont, and to forbear the navigation of these seas, without permission from the King of Spain.

To this Captain Hunt replied by repeating his former claim; by declaring that his orders were to keep possession; and by once more warning the Spaniards to depart.

The next month produced more protests and more replies, of which the tenour was nearly the same. The operations of such harmless enmity having produced no effect, were then reciprocally discontinued, and the English were left for a time to enjoy the pleasures of Falkland's Island without molestation.

This tranquillity, however, did not last long. A few months afterwards (June 4, 1770) the Industry, a Spanish frigate, commanded by an officer whose name was Madariaga, anchored in Port Egmont, bound, as was said, for Port Solidad, and reduced, by a passage from Buenos Ayres of fifty-three days, to want of water.

Three days afterwards four other frigates entered the port, and a broad pendant, such as is born by the commander of a naval armament, was displayed from the Industry. Captain Farmer of the Swift frigate, who commanded the garrison, ordered the crew of the Swift to come on shore, and assist in its defence; and directed Captain Maltby to bring the Favourite frigate, which he commanded, nearer to the land. The Spaniards easily discovering the purpose of his motion, let him know, that if he weighed his anchor, they would fire upon his ship; but paying no regard to these menaces, he advanced towards the shore. The Spanish fleet followed, and two shots were fired, which fell at a distance from him. He then sent to inquire the reason of such hostility, and was told that the shots were intended only as signals.

Both the English captains wrote the next day to Madariaga the

Thoughts on the Late Transactions respecting Falkland's Islands

Spanish commodore, warning him from the island, as from a place which the English held by right of discovery.

Madariaga, who seems to have had no desire of unnecessary mischief, invited them (June 9.) to send an officer who should take a view of his forces, that they might be convinced of the vanity of resistance, and do that without compulsion which he was upon refusal prepared to enforce.

An officer was sent, who found sixteen hundred men, with a train of twenty-seven cannon, four mortars, and two hundred bombs. The fleet consisted of five frigates from twenty to thirty guns, which were now stationed opposite to the Block-house.

He then sent them a formal memorial, in which he maintained his master's right to the whole Magellanick region, and exhorted the English to retire quietly from the settlement, which they could neither justify by right, nor maintain by power.

He offered them the liberty of carrying away whatever they were desirous to remove, and promised his receipt for what should be left, that no loss might be suffered by them.

His propositions were expressed in terms of great civility; but he concludes with demanding an answer in fifteen minutes.

Having while he was writing received the letters of warning written the day before by the English captains, he told them, that he thought himself able to prove the King of Spain's title to all those countries, but that this was no time for verbal altercations. He persisted in his determination, and allowed only fifteen minutes for an answer.

To this it was replied by Captain Farmer, that though there had been prescribed yet a shorter time, he should still resolutely defend his charge; that this, whether menace or force, would be considered as an insult on the British flag, and that satisfaction would certainly be required.

On the next day (June 10.) Madariaga landed his forces, and it may be easily imagined that he had no bloody conquest. The English had only a wooden blockhouse built at Woolwich, and carried in pieces to the island, with a small battery of cannon. To contend with obstinacy had been only to lavish life without use or hope. After the exchange of a very few shots, a capitulation was proposed.

The Spanish commander acted with moderation; he exerted

little of the conqueror; what he had offered before the attack, he granted after the victory; the English were allowed to leave the place with every honour, only their departure was delayed by the terms of the capitulation twenty days; and to secure their stay, the rudder of the Favourite was taken off. What they desired to carry away they removed without molestation; and of what they left an inventory was drawn, for which the Spanish officer by his receipt promised to be accountable.

Of this petty revolution, so sudden and so distant, the English ministry could not possibly have such notice as might enable them to prevent it. The conquest, if such it may be called, cost but three days; for the Spaniards, either supposing the garrison stronger than it was, or resolving to trust nothing to chance, or considering that as their force was greater, there was less danger of bloodshed, came with a power that made resistance ridiculous, and at once demanded and obtained possession.

The first account of any discontent expressed by the Spaniards was brought by Captain Hunt, who arriving at Plymouth June 3, 1770, informed the Admiralty that the island had been claimed in December by the governor of Port Solidad.

This claim, made by an officer of so little dignity, without any known direction from his superiors, could be considered only as the zeal or officiousness of an individual, unworthy of public notice or the formality of remonstrance.

In August Mr. Harris, the resident at Madrid, gave notice to Lord Weymouth of an account newly brought to Cadiz, that the English were in possession of Port Cuizada, the same which we call Port Egmont, in the Magellanick sea; that in January they had warned away two Spanish ships; and that an armament was sent out in May from Buenos Ayres to dislodge them.

It was perhaps not yet certain that this account was true; but the information, however faithful, was too late for prevention. It was easily known, that a fleet dispatched in May had before August succeeded or miscarried.

In October, Captain Maltby came to England, and gave the account which I have now epitomised, of his expulsion from Falkland's Islands.

From this moment the whole nation can witness that no time was lost. The navy was surveyed, the ships refitted, and comman-

Thoughts on the Late Transactions respecting Falkland's Islands

ders appointed; and a powerful fleet was assembled, well manned and well stored, with expedition after so long a peace perhaps never known before, and with vigour which after the waste of so long a war scarcely any other nation had been capable of exerting.

This preparation, so illustrious in the eyes of Europe, and so efficacious in its event, was obstructed by the utmost power of that noisy faction which has too long filled the kingdom, sometimes with the roar of empty menace, and sometimes with the yell of hypocritical lamentation. Every man saw, and every honest man saw with detestation, that they who desired to force their sovereign into war, endeavoured at the same time to disable him from action.

The vigour and spirit of the ministry easily broke through all the machinations of these pygmy rebels, and our armament was quickly such as was likely to make our negociations effectual.

The Prince of Masseran, in his first conference with the English ministers on this occasion, owned that he had from Madrid received intelligence that the English had been forcibly expelled from Falkland's Island by Buccarelli, the governor of Buenos Ayres, without any particular orders from the King of Spain. But being asked, whether in his master's name he disavowed Buccarelli's violence, he refused to answer without direction.

The scene of negociation was now removed to Madrid, and in September Mr. Harris was directed to demand from Grimaldi the Spanish minister the restitution of Falkland's Island, and a disavowal of Buccarelli's hostilities.

It was to be expected that Grimaldi would object to us our own behaviour, who had ordered the Spaniards to depart from the same island. To this it was replied, That the English forces were indeed directed to warn other nations away; but if compliance were refused, to proceed quietly in making their settlement, and suffer the subjects of whatever power to remain there without molestation. By possession thus taken, there was only a disputable claim advanced, which might be peaceably and regularly decided, without insult and without force; and if the Spaniards had complained at the British court, their reasons would have been heard, and all injuries redressed; but that, by presupposing the justice of their own title, and having recourse to arms, without any previous notice or remonstrance, they had violated the peace, and insulted the British government; and therefore it was expected that satisfaction should be made by publick disavowal and immediate restitution.

The answer of Grimaldi was ambiguous and cold. He did not allow that any particular orders had been given for driving the English from their settlement; but made no scruple of declaring, that such an ejection was nothing more than the settlers might have expected; and that Buccarelli had not, in his opinion, incurred any blame, as the general injunctions to the American governors were, to suffer no incroachments on the Spanish dominions.

In October the Prince of Masseran proposed a convention for the accommodation of differences by mutual concessions, in which the warning given to the Spaniards by Hunt should be disavowed on one side, and the violence used by Buccarelli on the other. This offer was considered as little less than a new insult, and Grimaldi was told, that injury required reparation; that when either party had suffered evident wrong, there was not the parity subsisting which is implied in conventions and contracts; that we considered ourselves as openly insulted, and demanded satisfaction plenary and unconditional.

Grimaldi affected to wonder that we were not yet appeased by their concessions. They had, he said, granted all that was required; they had offered to restore the island in the state in which they found it; but he thought that they likewise might hope for some regard, and that the warning sent by Hunt would be disavowed.

Mr. Harris, our minister at Madrid, insisted that the injured party had a right to unconditional reparation, and Grimaldi delayed his answer that a council might be called. In a few days orders were dispatched to Prince Masseran, by which he was commissioned to declare the King of Spain's readiness to satisfy the demands of the King of England, in expectation of receiving from him reciprocal satisfaction, by the disavowal, so often required, of Hunt's warning.

Finding the Spaniards disposed to make no other acknowledgments, the English ministry considered a war as not likely to be long avoided. In the latter end of November private notice was given of their danger to the merchants at Cadiz, and the officers absent from Gibraltar were remanded to their posts. Our naval

Thoughts on the Late Transactions respecting Falkland's Islands

force was every day increased, and we made no abatement of our original demand.

The obstinacy of the Spanish court still continued, and about the end of the year all hope of reconciliation was so nearly extinguished, that Mr. Harris was directed to withdraw, with the usual forms, from his residence at Madrid.

Moderation is commonly firm, and firmness is commonly successful; having not swelled our first requisition with any superfluous appendages, we had nothing to yield, we therefore only repeated our first proposition, prepared for war, though desirous of peace.

About this time, as is well known, the king of France dismissed Choiseul from his employments. What effect this revolution of the French court had upon the Spanish counsels, I pretend not to be informed. Choiseul had always professed pacific dispositions, nor is it certain, however it may be suspected, that he talked in different strains to different parties.

It seems to be almost the universal error of historians to suppose it politically, as it is physically true, that every effect has a proportionate cause. In the inanimate action of matter upon matter, the motion produced can be but equal to the force of the moving power; but the operations of life, whether private or publick, admit no such laws. The caprices of voluntary agents laugh at calculation. It is not always that there is a strong reason for a great event. Obstinacy and flexibility, malignity and kindness, give place alternately to each other, and the reason of these vicissitudes, however important may be the consequences, often escapes the mind in which the change is made.

Whether the alteration which began in January to appear in the Spanish counsels had any other cause than conviction of the impropriety of their past conduct, and of the danger of a new war, it is not easy to decide; but they began, whatever was the reason, to relax their haughtiness, and Mr. Harris's departure was countermanded.

The demands first made by England were still continued, and on January 22d, the prince of Masseran delivered a declaration, in which the king of Spain *disavows the violent enterprise* of Buccarelli, and promises *to restore the port and fort called Egmont, with all the artillery and stores, according to the inventory.*

Thoughts on the Late Transactions respecting Falkland's Islands

To this promise of restitution is subjoined that *this engagement to restore Port Egmont, cannot, nor ought in any wise to affect the question of the prior right of sovereignty of the Malouine otherwise called Falkland's Islands.*

This concession was accepted by the Earl of Rochford, who declared on the part of his master, that the Prince of Masseran being authorized by his Catholick Majesty, *to offer in his Majesty's name, to the King of Great Britain, a satisfaction for the injury done him by dispossessing him of Port Egmont,* and having signed a declaration expressing that his Catholick Majesty *disavows the expedition against Port Egmont,* and engages to restore it in the state in which it stood before the 10th of June 1770, *his Britannick majesty will look upon the said declaration, together with the full performance of the engagement on the part of his Catholick Majesty, as a satisfaction for the injury done to the crown of Great Britain.*

This is all that was originally demanded. The expedition is disavowed, and the island is restored. An injury is acknowledged by the reception of Lord Rochford's paper, who twice mentions the word *injury* and twice the word *satisfaction.*

The Spaniards have stipulated that the grant of possession shall not preclude the question of prior right, a question which we shall probably make no haste to discuss, and a right of which no formal resignation was ever required. This reserve has supplied matter for much clamour, and perhaps the English ministry would have been better pleased had the declaration been without it. But when we have obtained all that was asked, why should we complain that we have not more? When the possession is conceded, where is the evil that the right, which that concession supposes to be merely hypothetical, is referred to the Greek Calends for a future disquisition? Were the Switzers less free or less secure, because after their defection from the house of Austria they had never been declared independent before the treaty of Westphalia? Is the King of France less a sovereign because the King of England partakes his title?

If sovereignty implies undisputed right, scarce any prince is a sovereign through his whole dominions; if sovereignty consists in this, that no superiour is acknowledged, our King reigns at Port Egmont with sovereign authority. Almost every new acquired territory is in some degree controvertible, and till the controversy is decided, a term very difficult to be fixed, all that can be had is real possession and actual dominion.

This surely is a sufficient answer to the feudal gabble of a man who is every day lessening that splendour of character which once illuminated the kingdom, then dazzled, and afterwards inflamed it; and for whom it will be happy if the nation shall at last dismiss him to nameless obscurity with that equipoise of blame and praise which Corneille allows to Richlieu, a man who, I think, had much of his merit, and many of his faults.

> *Chacun parle a son gré de ce grand Cardinal,*
> *Mais pour moi je n'en dirai rien;*
> *Il m' a fait trop de bien pour en dire du mal,*
> *Il m' a fait trop de mal pour en dire du bien.*

To push advantages too far is neither generous nor just. Had we insisted on a concession of antecedent right, it may not misbecome us either as moralists or politicians, to consider what Grimaldi could have answered. We have already, he might say, granted you the whole effect of right, and have not denied you the name. We have not said that the right was ours before this concession, but only that what right we had, is not by this concession vacated. We have now for more than two centuries ruled large tracts of the American continent, by a claim which perhaps is valid only upon this consideration, that no power can produce a better; by the right of discovery and prior settlement. And by such titles almost all the dominions of the earth are holden, except that their original is beyond memory, and greater obscurity gives them greater veneration. Should we allow this plea to be annulled, the whole fabrick of our empire shakes at the foundation. When you suppose yourselves to have first descried the disputed island, you suppose what you can hardly prove. We were at least the general discoverers of the Magellanick region, and have hitherto held it with all its adjacencies. The justice of this tenure the world has hitherto admitted, and yourselves at least tacitly allowed it, when about twenty years ago you desisted from your purposed expedition, and expressly disowned any design of settling, where you are now not content to settle and to reign, without extorting such a confession of original right, as may invite every other nation to follow you.

Thoughts on the Late Transactions respecting Falkland's Islands

To considerations such as these, it is reasonable to impute that anxiety of the Spaniards, from which the importance of this island is inferred by Junius, one of the few writers of his despicable faction whose name does not disgrace the page of an opponent. The value of the thing disputed may be very different to him that gains and him that loses it. The Spaniards, by yielding Falkland's island, have admitted a precedent of what they think encroachment; have suffered a breach to be made in the outworks of their empire; and notwithstanding the reserve of prior right, have suffered a dangerous exception to the prescriptive tenure of their American territories.

Such is the loss of Spain; let us now compute the profit of Britain. We have, by obtaining a disavowal of Buccarelli's expedition, and a restitution of our settlement, maintained the honour of the crown, and the superiority of our influence. Beyond this what have we acquired? What, but a bleak and gloomy solitude, an island thrown aside from human use, stormy in winter, and barren in summer; an island which not the southern savages have dignified with habitation; where a garrison must be kept in a state that contemplates with envy the exiles of Siberia; of which the expence will be perpetual, and the use only occasional; and which, if fortune smile upon our labours, may become a nest of smugglers in peace, and in war the refuge of future Buccaniers. To all this the Government has now given ample attestation, for the island has been since abandoned, and perhaps was kept only to quiet clamours, with an intention, not then wholly concealed, of quitting it in a short time.

This is the country of which we have now possession, and of which a numerous party pretends to wish that we had murdered thousands for the titular sovereignty. To charge any men with such madness, approaches to an accusation defeated by its own incredibility. As they have been long accumulating falsehoods, it is possible that they are now only adding another to the heap, and that they do not mean all that they profess. But of this faction what evil may not be credited? They have hitherto shewn no virtue, and very little wit, beyond that mischievous cunning for which it is held by Hale that children may be hanged.

As war is the last of remedies, *cuncta prius tentanda*, all lawful expedients must be used to avoid it. As war is the extremity of

Thoughts on the Late Transactions respecting Falkland's Islands

evil, it is surely the duty of those whose station intrusts them with the care of nations, to avert it from their charge. There are diseases of animal nature which nothing but amputation can remove; so there may, by the depravation of human passions, be sometimes a gangrene in collective life for which fire and the sword are the necessary remedies; but in what can skill or caution be better shewn than preventing such dreadful operations, while there is yet room for gentler methods?

It is wonderful with what coolness and indifference the greater part of mankind see war commenced. Those that hear of it at a distance, or read of it in books, but have never presented its evils to their minds, consider it as little more than a splendid game, a proclamation, an army, a battle, and a triumph. Some indeed must perish in the most successful field, but they die upon the bed of honour, *resign their lives amidst the joys of conquest, and, filled with England's glory, smile in death.*

The life of a modern soldier is ill represented by heroick fiction. War has means of destruction more formidable than the cannon and the sword. Of the thousands and ten thousands that perished in our late contests with France and Spain, a very small part ever felt the stroke of an enemy; the rest languished in tents and ships, amidst damps and putrefaction; pale, torpid, spiritless, and helpless; gasping and groaning, unpitied among men, made obdurate by long continuance of hopeless misery; and were at last whelmed in pits, or heaved into the ocean, without notice and without remembrance. By incommodious encampments and unwholesome stations, where courage is useless, and enterprise impracticable, fleets are silently dispeopled, and armies sluggishly melted away.

This is a people gradually exhausted, for the most part with little effect. The wars of civilized nations make very slow changes in the system of empire. The public perceives scarcely any alteration but an increase of debt; and the few individuals who are benefited, are not supposed to have the clearest right to their advantages. If he that shared the danger enjoyed the profit, and after bleeding in the battle grew rich by the victory, he might shew his gains without envy. But at the conclusion of a ten years war, how are we recompensed for the death of multitudes and the expence of millions, but by contemplating the sudden glories of paymasters and agents, contractors and commissaries, whose equipages shine like meteors, and whose palaces rise like exhalations.

These are the men who, without virtue, labour, or hazard, are growing rich as their country is impoverished; they rejoice when obstinacy or ambition adds another year to slaughter and devastation; and laugh from their desks at bravery and science, while they are adding figure to figure, and cipher to cipher, hoping for a new contract from a new armament, and computing the profits of a siege or tempest.

Those who suffer their minds to dwell on these considerations will think it no great crime in the ministry that they have not snatched with eagerness the first opportunity of rushing into the field, when they were able to obtain by quiet negociation all the real good that victory could have brought us.

Of victory indeed every nation is confident before the sword is drawn; and this mutual confidence produces that wantonness of bloodshed that has so often desolated the world. But it is evident, that of contradictory opinions one must be wrong, and the history of mankind does not want examples that may teach caution to the daring, and moderation to the proud.

Let us not think our laurels blasted by condescending to inquire, whether we might not possibly grow rather less than greater by attacking Spain. Whether we should have to contend with Spain alone, whatever has been promised by our patriots, may very reasonably be doubted. A war declared for the empty sound of an ancient title to a Magellanick rock would raise the indignation of the earth against us. These encroachers on the waste of nature, says our ally the Russian, if they succeed in their first effort of usurpation, will make war upon us for a title to Kamschatscha. These universal settlers, says our ally the Dane, will in a short time settle upon Greenland, and a fleet will batter Copenhagen, till we are willing to confess that it always was their own.

In a quarrel like this, it is not possible that any power should favour us, and it is very likely that some would oppose us. The French, we are told, are otherwise employed; the contests between the King of France and his own subjects are sufficient to withold him from supporting Spain. But who does not know that a foreign war has often put a stop to civil discords? It withdraws the attention of the publick from domestick grievances, and affords

Thoughts on the Late Transactions respecting Falkland's Islands

opportunities of dismissing the turbulent and restless to distant employments. The Spaniards have always an argument of irresistible persuasion. If France will not support them against England, they will strengthen England against France.

But let us indulge a dream of idle speculation, and suppose that we are to engage with Spain, and with Spain alone; it is not even yet very certain that much advantage will be gained. Spain is not easily vulnerable; her kingdom, by the loss or cession of many fragments of dominion, is become solid and compact. The Spaniards have indeed no fleet able to oppose us, but they will not endeavour actual opposition; they will shut themselves up in their own territories, and let us exhaust our seamen in a hopeless siege. They will give commissions to privateers of every nation, who will prey upon our merchants without possibility of reprisal. If they think their plate fleet in danger, they will forbid it to set sail, and live a while upon the credit of treasure which all Europe knows to be safe; and which, if our obstinacy should continue till they can no longer be without it, will be conveyed to them with secrecy and security by our natural enemies the French, or by the Dutch our natural allies.

But the whole continent of Spanish America will lie open to invasion; we shall have nothing to do but march into these wealthy regions, and make their present masters confess that they were always ours by ancient right. We shall throw brass and iron out of our houses, and nothing but silver will be seen among us.

All this is very desirable, but it is not certain that it can be easily attained. Large tracts of America were added by the last war to the British dominions; but, if the faction credit their own Apollo, they were conquered in Germany. They at best are only the barren parts of the continent, the refuse of the earlier adventurers, which the French, who came last, had taken only as better than nothing.

Against the Spanish dominions we have never hitherto been able to do much. A few privateers have grown rich at their expence, but no scheme of conquest has yet been successful. They are defended not by walls mounted with cannons which by cannons may be battered, but by the storms of the deep and the vapours of the land, by the flames of calenture and blasts of pestilence.

In the reign of Elizabeth, the favourite period of English greatness, no enterprises against America had any other consequence than that of extending English navigation. Here Cavendish perished after all his hazards; and here Drake and Hawkins, great as they were in knowledge and in fame, having promised honour to themselves and dominion to the country, sunk by desperation and misery in dishonourable graves.

During the protectorship of Cromwell, a time of which the patriotick tribes still more ardently desire the return, the Spanish dominions were again attempted; but here, and only here, the fortune of Cromwell made a pause. His forces were driven from Hispaniola, his hopes of possessing the West Indies vanished, and Jamaica was taken, only that the whole expedition might not grow ridiculous.

The attack of Carthagena is yet remembered, where the Spaniards from the ramparts saw their invaders destroyed by the hostility of the elements; poisoned by the air, and crippled by the dews; where every hour swept away battalions; and in the three days that passed between the descent and re-embarkation, half an army perished.

In the last war the Havanna was taken, at what expence is too well remembered. May my country be never cursed with such another conquest!

These instances of miscarriage, and these arguments of difficulty, may perhaps abate the military ardour of the Publick. Upon the opponents of the government their operation will be different; they wish for war, but not for conquest; victory would defeat their purposes equally with peace, because prosperity would naturally continue trust in those hands which had used it fortunately. The patriots gratified themselves with expectations that some sinistrous accident, or erroneous conduct, might diffuse discontent and inflame malignity. Their hope is malevolence, and their good is evil.

Of their zeal for their country we have already had a specimen. While they were terrifying the nation with doubts whether it was any longer to exist; while they represented invasive armies as hovering in the clouds, and hostile fleets as emerging from the deeps; they obstructed our levies of seamen, and embarrassed our endeavours of defence. Of such men he thinks with unnecessary candour who does not believe them likely to have promoted the miscarriage which they desired, by intimidating our troops or betraying our counsels.

It is considered as an injury to the Publick by those sanguinary statesmen, that though the fleet has been refitted and manned, yet no hostilities have followed; and they who sat wishing for misery and slaughter are disappointed of their pleasure. But as peace is the end of war, it is the end likewise of preparations for war; and he may be justly hunted down as the enemy of mankind, that can chuse to snatch by violence and bloodshed, what gentler means can equally obtain.

The ministry are reproached as not daring to provoke an enemy, lest ill success should discredit and displace them. I hope that they had better reasons; that they paid some regard to equity and humanity; and considered themselves as entrusted with the safety of their fellow-subjects, and as the destroyers of all that should be superfluously slaughtered. But let us suppose that their own safety had some influence on their conduct, they will not, however, sink to a level with their enemies. Though the motive might be selfish, the act was innocent. They who grow rich by administering physick, are not to be numbered with them that get money by dispensing poison. If they maintain power by harmlessness and peace, they must for ever be at a great distance from ruffians who would gain it by mischief and confusion. The watch of a city may guard it for hire; but are well employed in protecting it from those who lie in wait to fire the streets and rob the houses amidst the conflagration.

An unsuccessful war would undoubtedly have had the effect which the enemies of the Ministry so earnestly desire; for who could have sustained the disgrace of folly ending in misfortune? But had wanton invasion undeservedly prospered, had Falkland's Island been yielded unconditionally with every right prior and posterior; though the rabble might have shouted, and the windows have blazed, yet those who know the value of life, and the uncertainty of publick credit, would have murmured, perhaps unheard, at the increase of our debt and the loss of our people.

This thirst of blood, however the visible promoters of sedition may think it convenient to shrink from the accusation, is loudly avowed by Junius, the writer to whom his party owes much of its pride, and some of its popularity. Of Junius it cannot be said, as of

Thoughts on the Late Transactions respecting Falkland's Islands

Ulysses, that he scatters ambigious expressions among the vulgar; for he cries *havock* without reserve, and endeavours to let slip the dogs of foreign or of civil war, ignorant whither they are going, and careless what may be their prey.

Junius has sometimes made his satire felt, but let not injudicious admiration mistake the venom of the shaft for the vigour of the bow. He has sometimes sported with lucky malice; but to him that knows his company, it is not hard to be sarcastick in a mask. While he walks like Jack the Giant-killer in a coat of darkness, he may do much mischief with little strength. Novelty captivates the superficial and thoughtless; vehemence delights the discontented and turbulent. He that contradicts acknowledged truth will always have an audience; he that vilifies established authority will always find abettors.

Junius burst into notice with a blaze of impudence which has rarely glared upon the world before, and drew the rabble after him as a monster makes a show. When he had once provided for his safety by impenetrable secrecy, he had nothing to combat but truth and justice, enemies whom he knows to be feeble in the dark. Being then at liberty to indulge himself in all the immunities of invisibility; out of the reach of danger, he has been bold; out of the reach of shame, he has been confident. As a rhetorician, he has had the art of persuading when he seconded desire; as a reasoner, he has convinced those who had no doubt before; as a moralist, he has taught that virtue may disgrace; and as a patriot, he has gratified the mean by insults on the high. Finding sedition ascendant, he has been able to advance it; finding the nation combustible, he has been able to inflame it. Let us abstract from his wit the vivacity of insolence, and withdraw from his efficacy the sympathetick favour of Plebeian malignity; I do not say that we shall leave him nothing; the cause that I defend scorns the help of falsehood; but if we leave him only his merit, what will be his praise?

It is not by his liveliness of imagery, his pungency of periods, or his fertility of allusion, that he detains the cits of London, and the boors of Middlesex. Of style and sentiment they take no cognizance. They admire him for virtues like their own, for contempt of order and violence of outrage, for rage of defamation and audacity of falsehood. The Supporters of the Bill of Rights feel

Thoughts on the Late Transactions respecting Falkland's Islands

no niceties of composition, nor dexterities of sophistry; their faculties are better proportioned to the bawl of Bellas, or barbarity of Beckford; but they are told that Junius is on their side, and they are therefore sure that Junius is infallible. Those who know not whither he would lead them, resolve to follow him; and those who cannot find his meaning, hope he means rebellion.

Junius is an unusual phænomenon, on which some have gazed with wonder and some with terrour, but wonder and terrour are transitory passions. He will soon be more closely viewed or more attentively examined, and what folly has taken for a comet that from its flaming hair shook pestilence and war, inquiry will find to be only a meteor formed by the vapours of putrefying democracy, and kindled into flame by the effervescence of interest struggling with conviction; which after having plunged its followers in a bog, will leave us inquiring why we regarded it.

Yet though I cannot think the style of Junius secure from criticism, though his expressions are often trite, and his periods feeble, I should never have stationed him where he has placed himself, had I not rated him by his morals rather than his faculties. What, says Pope, must be the priest, where a monkey is the God? What must be the drudge of a party of which the heads are Wilkes and Crosby, Sawbridge and Townsend?

Junius knows his own meaning and can therefore tell it. He is an enemy to the ministry, he sees them growing hourly stronger. He knows that a war at once unjust and unsuccessful would have certainly displaced them, and is therefore, in his zeal for his country, angry that war was not unjustly made, and unsuccessfully conducted. But there are others whose thoughts are less clearly expressed, and whose schemes perhaps are less consequentially digested; who declare that they do not wish for a rupture, yet condemn the ministry for not doing that, by which a rupture would naturally have been made.

If one party resolves to demand what the other resolves to refuse, the dispute can be determined only by arbitration; and between powers who have no common superiour, there is no other arbitrator than the sword.

Whether the ministry might not equitably have demanded more, is not worth a question. The utmost exertion of right is always invidious, and where claims are not easily determinable is always

Thoughts on the Late Transactions respecting Falkland's Islands

dangerous. We asked all that was necessary, and persisted in our first claim without mean recession, or wanton aggravation. The Spaniards found us resolute, and complied after a short struggle.

The real crime of the ministry is, that they have found the means of avoiding their own ruin; but the charge against them is multifarious and confused, as will happen, when malice and discontent are ashamed of their complaint. The past and the future are complicated in the censure. We have heard a tumultuous clamour about honour and rights, injuries and insults, the British flag, and the Favourite's rudder, Buccarelli's conduct, and Grimaldi's declarations, the Manilla ransom, delays and reparation.

Through the whole argument of the faction runs the general errour, that our settlement on Falkland's Island was not only lawful but unquestionable; that our right was not only certain but acknowledged; and that the equity of our conduct was such, that the Spaniards could not blame or obstruct it without combating their own conviction, and opposing the general opinion of mankind.

If once it be discovered that, in the opinion of the Spaniards, our settlement was usurped, our claim arbitrary, and our conduct insolent, all that has happened will appear to follow by a natural concatenation. Doubts will produce disputes and disquisition, disquisition requires delay, and delay causes inconvenience.

Had the Spanish government immediately yielded unconditionally all that was required, we might have been satisfied; but what would Europe have judged of their submission? That they shrunk before us as a conquered people, who having lately yielded to our arms, were now compelled to sacrifice to our pride. The honour of the Publick is indeed of high importance; but we must remember that we have had to transact with a mighty King and a powerful nation, who have unluckily been taught to think that they have honour to keep or lose as well as ourselves.

When the Admiralty were told in June of the warning given to Hunt, they were, I suppose, informed that Hunt had first provoked it by warning away the Spaniards, and naturally considered one act of insolence as balanced by another, without expecting that more would be done on either side. Of representations and remonstrances there would be no end, if they were to be made whenever small commanders are uncivil to each other; nor could peace ever be enjoyed, if upon such transient provocations it be

Thoughts on the Late Transactions respecting Falkland's Islands

imagined necessary to prepare for war. We might then, it is said, have increased our force with more leisure and less inconvenience; but this is to judge only by the event. We omitted to disturb the Publick, because we did not suppose that an armament would be necessary.

Some months afterwards, as has been told, Buccarelli, the governor of Buenos Ayres, sent against the settlement of Port Egmont a force which ensured the conquest. The Spanish commander required the English captains to depart, but they thinking that resistance necessary which they knew to be useless, gave the Spaniards, the right of prescribing terms of capitulation. The Spaniards imposed no new condition except that the sloop should not sail under twenty days; and of this they secured the performance by taking off the rudder.

To an inhabitant of the land there appears nothing in all this unreasonable or offensive. If the English intended to keep their stipulation, how were they injured by the detention of the rudder? If the rudder be to a ship what his tail is in fables to a fox, the part in which honour is placed, and of which the violation is never to be endured, I am sorry that the *Favourite* suffered an indignity, but cannot yet think it a cause for which nations should slaughter one another.

When Buccarelli's invasion was known, and the dignity of the crown infringed, we demanded reparation and prepared for war, and we gained equal respect by the moderation of our terms, and the spirit of our exertion. The Spanish minister immediately denied that Buccarelli had received any particular orders to seize Port Egmont, nor pretended that he was justified otherwise than by the general instructions by which the American governors are required to exclude the subjects of other powers.

To have inquired whether our settlement at Port Egmont was any violation of the Spanish rights, had been to enter upon a discussion which the pertinacity of political disputants might have continued without end. We therefore called for restitution, not as a confession of right, but as a reparation of honour, which required that we should be restored to our former state upon the island, and that the King of Spain should disavow the action of his governor.

In return to this demand, the Spaniards expected from us a

disavowal of the menaces with which they had been first insulted by Hunt; and if the claim to the island be supposed doubtful, they certainly expected it with equal reason. This, however, was refused, and our superiority of strength gave validity to our arguments.

But we are told that the disavowal of the King of Spain is temporary and fallacious; that Buccarelli's armament had all the appearance of regular forces and a concerted expedition; and that he is not treated at home as a man guilty of piracy, or as disobedient to the orders of his master.

That the expedition was well planned, and the forces properly supplied, affords no proof of communication between the governor and his court. Those who are intrusted with the care of kingdoms in another hemisphere, must always be trusted with power to defend them.

As little can be inferred from his reception at the Spanish court. He is not punished indeed, for what has he done that deserves punishment? He was sent into America to govern and defend the dominions of Spain. He thought the English were encroaching, and drove them away. No Spaniard thinks that he has exceeded his duty, nor does the King of Spain charge him with excess. The boundaries of dominion in that part of the world have not yet been settled; and he mistook, if a mistake there was, like a zealous subject, in his master's favour.

But all this inquiry is superfluous. Considered as a reparation of honour, the disavowal of the King of Spain, made in the sight of all Europe, is of equal value, whether true or false. There is indeed no reason to question its veracity; they, however, who do not believe it, must allow the weight of that influence by which a great prince is reduced to disown his own commission.

But the general orders upon which the governor is acknowledged to have acted, are neither disavowed nor explained. Why the Spaniards should disavow the defence of their own territories, the warmest disputant will find it difficult to tell; and if by an explanation is meant an accurate delineation of the southern empire, and the limitation of their claims beyond the line, it cannot be imputed to any very culpable remissness, that what has been denied for two centuries to the European powers, was not obtained in a hasty wrangle about a petty settlement.

Thoughts on the Late Transactions respecting Falkland's Islands

The ministry were too well acquainted with negociation to fill their heads with such idle expectations. The question of right was inexplicable and endless. They left it as it stood. To be restored to actual possession was easily practicable. This restoration they required and obtained.

But they should, say their opponents, have insisted upon more; they should have exacted not only reparation of our honour but repayment of our expence. Nor are they all satisfied with the recovery of the costs and damages of the present contest; they are for taking this opportunity of calling in old debts, and reviving our right to the ransom of Manilla.

The Manilla ransom has, I think, been most mentioned by the inferior bellowers of sedition. Those who lead the faction know that it cannot be remembered much to their advantage. The followers of Lord Rockingham remember that his ministry begun and ended without obtaining it; the adherents to Grenville would be told, that he could never be taught to understand our claim. The law of nations made little of his knowledge. Let him not, however, be depreciated in his grave. If he was sometimes wrong, he was often right.

Of reimbursement the talk has been more confident, though not more reasonable. The expences of war have been often desired, have been sometimes required, but were never paid; or never, but when resistance was hopeless, and there remained no choice between submission and destruction.

Of our late equipments I know not from whom the charge can be very properly expected. The king of Spain disavows the violence which provoked us to arm, and for the mischiefs which he did not do, why should he pay? Buccarelli, though he had learned all the arts of an East-Indian governor, could hardly have collected at Buenos Ayres a sum sufficient to satisfy our demands. If he be honest, he is hardly rich; and if he be disposed to rob, he has the misfortune of being placed where robbers have been before him.

The king of Spain indeed delayed to comply with our proposals, and our armament was made necessary by unsatisfactory answers and dilatory debates. The delay certainly increased our expences, and it is not unlikely that the increase of our expences put an end to the delay.

But this is the inevitable process of human affairs. Negociation

Thoughts on the Late Transactions respecting Falkland's Islands

requires time. What is not apparent to intuition must be found by inquiry. Claims that have remained doubtful for ages cannot be settled in a day. Reciprocal complaints are not easily adjusted but by reciprocal compliance. The Spaniards thinking themselves entitled to the island, and injured by Captain Hunt, in their turn demanded satisfaction, which was refused; and where is the wonder if their concessions were delayed! They may tell us, that an independent nation is to be influenced not by command, but by persuasion; that if we expect our proposals to be received without deliberation, we assume that sovereignty which they do not grant us; and that if we arm while they are deliberating, we must indulge our martial ardour at our own charge.

The English ministry asked all that was reasonable, and enforced all that they asked. Our national honour is advanced, and our interest, if any interest we have, is sufficiently secured. There can be none amongst us to whom this transaction does not seem happily concluded, but those who having fixed their hopes on public calamities, sat like vultures waiting for a day of carnage. Having worn out all the arts of domestick sedition, having wearied violence, and exhausted falsehood, they yet flattered themselves with some assistance from the pride or malice of Spain; and when they could no longer make the people complain of grievances which they did not feel, they had the comfort yet of knowing that real evils were possible, and their resolution is well known of charging all evil on their governours.

The reconciliation was therefore considered as the loss of their last anchor; and received not only with the fretfulness of disappointment but the rage of desparation. When they found that all were happy in spite of their machinations, and the soft effulgence of peace shone out upon the nation, they felt no motion but that of sullen envy; they could not, like Milton's prince of hell, abstract themselves a moment from their evil; as they have not the wit of Satan, they have not his virtue; they tried once again what could be done by sophistry without art, and confidence without credit. They represented their Sovereign as dishonoured and their country as betrayed, or, in their fiercer paroxysms of fury, reviled their Sovereign as betraying it.

Their pretences I have here endeavoured to expose, by showing that more than has been yielded was not to be expected, that more

Thoughts on the Late Transactions respecting Falkland's Islands

perhaps was not to be desired, and that if all had been refused, there had scarcely been an adequate reason for a war.

There was perhaps never much danger of war or of refusal, but what danger there was, proceeded from the faction. Foreign nations, unacquainted with the insolence of Common Councils, and unaccustomed to the howl of Plebeian patriotism, when they heard of rabbles and riots, of petitions and remonstrances, of discontent in Surrey, Derbyshire, and Yorkshire, when they saw the chain of subordination broken, and the legislature threatened and defied, naturally imagined that such a government had little leisure for Falkland's Island; they supposed that the English when they returned ejected from Port Egmont, would find Wilkes invested with the protectorate; or see the mayor of London, what the French have formerly seen their mayors of the palace, the commander of the army and tutor of the King; that they would be called to tell their tale before the Common Council; and that the world was to expect war or peace from a vote of the subscribers to the Bill of Rights.

But our enemies have now lost their hopes, and our friends I hope are recovered from their fears. To fancy that our government can be subverted by the rabble, whom its lenity has pampered into impudence, is to fear that a city may be drowned by the overflowing of its kennels. The distemper which cowardice or malice thought either decay of the vitals, or resolution of the nerves, appears at last to have been nothing more than a political *phthiriasis* a disease too loathsome for a plainer name; but the effect of negligence rather than of weakness, and of which the shame is greater than the danger.

Among the disturbers of our quiet are some animals of greater bulk, whom their power of roaring persuaded us to think formidable, but we now perceive that sound and force do not always go together. The noise of a savage proves nothing but his hunger.

After all our broils, foreign and domestick, we may at last hope to remain awhile in quiet, amused with the view of our own success. We have gained political strength by the increase of our reputation; we have gained real strength by the reparation of our navy; we have shewn Europe that ten years of war have not yet exhausted us; and we have enforced our settlement on an island on which twenty years ago we durst not venture to look.

Thoughts on the Late Transactions respecting Falkland's Islands

These are the gratifications only of honest minds; but there is a time in which hope comes to all. From the present happiness of the publick the patriots themselves may derive advantage. To be harmless though by impotence obtains some degree of kindness; no man hates a worm as he hates a viper; they were once dreaded enough to be detested, as serpents that could bite; they have now shewn that they can only hiss, and may therefore quietly slink into holes, and change their slough unmolested and forgotten.

7
The Patriot
(1774)

To improve the golden moment of opportunity, and catch the good that is within our reach, is the great art of life. Many wants are suffered, which might once have been supplied; and much time is lost in regretting the time which had been lost before.

At the end of every seven years comes the Saturnalian season, when the freemen of Great Britain may please themselves with the choice of their representatives. This happy day has now arrived, somewhat sooner than it could be claimed.

To select and depute those, by whom laws are to be made, and taxes to be granted, is a high dignity and an important trust: and it is the business of every elector to consider, how this dignity may be well sustained, and this trust faithfully discharged.

It ought to be deeply impressed on the minds of all who have voices in this national deliberation, that no man can deserve a seat in parliament who is not a PATRIOT. No other man will protect our rights, no other man can merit our confidence.

A Patriot is he whose public conduct is regulated by one single motive, the love of his country; who, as an agent in parliament, has for himself neither hope nor fear, neither kindness nor resentment, but refers every thing to the common interest.

That of five hundred men, such as this degenerate age affords, a majority can be found thus virtuously abstracted, who will affirm? Yet there is no good in despondence: vigilance and activity often effect more than was expected. Let us take a Patriot where we can meet him; and that we may not flatter ourselves by false appearances, distinguish those marks which are certain, from those which may deceive: for a man may have the external appearance of a Patriot, without the constituent qualities; as false coins have often lustre, tho' they want weight.

The Patriot

Some claim a place in the list of Patriots by an acrimonious and unremitting opposition to the Court.

This mark is by no means infallible. Patriotism is not necessarily included in rebellion. A man may hate his King, yet not love his Country. He that has been refused a reasonable or unreasonable request, who thinks his merit under-rated, and sees his influence declining, begins soon to talk of natural equality, the absurdity of *many made for one*, the original compact, the foundation of authority, and the majesty of the people. As his political melancholy increases, he tells, and perhaps dreams of the advances of the prerogative, and the dangers of arbitrary power; yet his design in all his declamation is not to benefit his country, but to gratify his malice.

These, however, are the most honest of the opponents of government; their patriotism is a species of disease; and they feel some part of what they express. But the greater, far the greater number of those who rave and rail, and inquire and accuse, neither suspect nor fear, nor care for the Public; but hope to force their way to riches by virulence and invective, and are vehement and clamorous, only that they may be sooner hired to be silent.

A man sometimes starts up a Patriot, only by disseminating discontent and propagating reports of secret influence, of dangerous counsels, of violated rights and encroaching usurpation.

This practice is no certain note of Patriotism. To instigate the populace with rage beyond the provocation, is to suspend public happiness, if not to destroy it. He is no lover of his country, that unnecessarily disturbs its peace. Few errors, and few faults of government can justify an appeal to the rabble; who ought not to judge of what they cannot understand, and whose opinions are not propagated by reason, but caught by contagion.

The fallaciousness of this note of patriotism is particularly apparent, when the clamour continues after the evil is past. They who are still filling our ears with Mr. Wilkes, and the Freeholders of Middlesex, lament a grievance, that is now at an end. Mr. Wilkes may be chosen, if any will choose him, and the precedent of his exclusion makes not any honest, or any decent man, think himself in danger.

It may be doubted whether the name of a Patriot can be fairly given as the reward of secret satire, or open outrage. To fill the

The Patriot

news-papers with sly hints of corruption and intrigue, to circulate the Middlesex Journal and London Pacquet, may indeed be zeal; but it may likewise be interest and malice. To offer a petition, not expected to be granted; to insult a King with a rude remonstrance, only because there is no punishment for legal insolence, is not courage, for there is no danger; nor patriotism, for it tends to the subversion of order, and lets wickedness loose upon the land, by destroying the reverence due to sovereign authority.

It is the quality of Patriotism to be jealous and watchful, to observe all secret machinations, and to see public dangers at a distance. The true *Lover of his country* is ready to communicate his fears and to sound the alarm, whenever he perceives the approach of mischief. But he sounds no alarm, when there is no enemy: he never terrifies his countrymen till he is terrified himself. The patriotism therefore may be justly doubted of him, who professes to be disturbed by incredibilities; who tells, that the last peace was obtained by bribing the Princess of Wales; that the King is grasping at arbitrary power; and that because the French in the new conquests enjoy their own laws, there is a design at court of abolishing in England the trial by juries.

Still less does the true Patriot circulate opinions which he knows to be false. No man, who loves his country, fills the nation with clamorous complaints, that the Protestant religion is in danger, because *Popery is established in the extensive province of Quebec*, a falsehood so open and shameless, that it can need no confutation among those who know that of which it is almost impossible for the most unenlightened zealot to be ignorant,

That Quebec is on the other side of the Atlantic, at too great a distance to do much good or harm to the European world:

That the inhabitants, being French, were always Papists, who are certainly more dangerous as enemies, than as subjects:

That though the province be wide, the people are few, probably not so many as may be found in one of the larger English counties:

That persecution is not more virtuous in a Protestant than a Papist; and that while we blame Lewis the Fourteenth, for his dragoons and his gallies, we ought, when power comes into our hands, to use it with greater equity:

That when Canada with its inhabitants was yielded, the free enjoyment of their religion was stipulated; a condition, of which

The Patriot

King William, who was no propagator of Popery, gave an example nearer home, at the surrender of Limerick:
That in an age, where every mouth is open for *liberty of conscience*, it is equitable to shew some regard to the conscience of a Papist, who may be supposed, like other men, to think himself safest in his own religion; and that those at least, who enjoy a toleration, ought not to deny it to our new subjects.

If liberty of conscience be a natural right, we have no power to with-hold it; if it be an indulgence, it may be allowed to Papists, while it is not denied to other sects.

A Patriot is necessarily and invariably a lover of the people. But even this mark may sometimes deceive us.

The people is a very heterogeneous and confused mass of the wealthy and the poor, the wise and the foolish, the good and the bad. Before we confer on a man, who caresses the people, the title of Patriot, we must examine to what part of the people he directs his notice. It is proverbially said, that he who dissembles his own character, may be known by that of his companions. If the candidate of Patriotism endeavours to infuse right opinions into the higher ranks, and by their influence to regulate the lower; if he consorts chiefly with the wise, the temperate, the regular, and the virtuous, his love of the people may be rational and honest. But if his first or principal application be to the indigent, who are always inflammable; to the weak, who are naturally suspicious; to the ignorant, who are easily misled; and to the profligate, who have no hope but from mischief and confusion; let his love of the people be no longer boasted. No man can reasonably be thought a lover of his country, for roasting an ox, or burning a boot, or attending the meeting at Mile-End, or registering his name in the Lumber-Troop. He may, among the drunkards be a *hearty fellow*, and among sober handicraftsmen, a *free-spoken gentleman*; but he must have some better distinction before he is a *Patriot*.

A Patriot is always ready to countenance the just claims, and animate the reasonable hopes of the people; he reminds them frequently of their rights, and stimulates them to resent encroachments, and to multiply securities.

But all this may be done in appearance, without real patriotism. He that raises false hopes to serve a present purpose, only makes a way for disappointment and discontent. He who promises to

The Patriot

endeavour, what he knows his endeavours unable to effect, means only to delude his followers by an empty clamour of ineffectual zeal.

A true Patriot is no lavish promiser: he undertakes not to shorten parliaments; to repeal laws; or to change the mode of representation, transmitted by our ancestors: he knows that futurity is not in his power, and that all times are not alike favourable to change.

Much less does he make a vague and indefinite promise of obeying the mandates of his constituents. He knows the prejudices of faction, and the inconstancy of the multitude. He would first inquire, how the opinion of his constituents shall be taken. Popular instructions are commonly the work, not of the wise and steady, but the violent and rash; meetings held for directing representatives are seldom attended but by the idle and the dissolute; and he is not without suspicion, that of his constituents, as of other numbers of men, the smaller part may often be the wiser.

He considers himself as deputed to promote the publick good, and to preserve his constituents, with the rest of his countrymen, not only from being hurt by others, but from hurting themselves.

The common marks of patriotism having been examined, and shewn to be such as artifice may counterfeit, or folly misapply, it cannot be improper to consider, whether there are not some characteristical modes of speaking or acting, which may prove a man to be NOT A PATRIOT.

In this inquiry, perhaps clearer evidence may be discovered, and firmer persuasion attained; for it is commonly easier to know what is wrong than what is right; to find what we should avoid, than what we should pursue.

As war is one of the heaviest of national evils, a calamity, in which every species of misery is involved; as it sets the general safety to hazard, suspends commerce, and desolates the country; as it exposes great numbers to hardships, dangers, captivity, and death; no man, who desires the publick prosperity, will inflame general resentment by aggravating minute injuries, or enforcing disputable rights of little importance.

It may therefore be safely pronounced, that those men are no Patriots, who when the national honour was vindicated in the sight of Europe, and the Spaniards having invaded what they call their own, had shrunk to a disavowal of their attempt and a relaxation

The Patriot

of their claim, would still have instigated us to a war for a bleak and barren spot in the Magellanic ocean, of which no use could be made unless it were a place of exile for the hypocrites of patriotism.

Yet let it not be forgotten, that by the howling violence of patriotic rage, the nation was for a time exasperated to such madness, that for a barren rock, under a stormy sky, we might have now been fighting and dying, had not our competitors been wiser than ourselves; and those who are now courting the favour of the people by noisy professions of public spirit, would, while they were counting the profits of their artifice, have enjoyed the patriotic pleasure of hearing sometimes, that thousands had been slaughtered in a battle, and sometimes that a navy had been dispeopled by poisoned air and corrupted food.

He that wishes to see his country robbed of its rights, cannot be a Patriot.

That man therefore is no Patriot, who justifies the ridiculous claims of American usurpation; who endeavours to deprive the nation of its natural and lawful authority over its own colonies; those colonies, which were settled under English protection; were constituted by an English charter; and have been defended by English arms.

To suppose, that by sending out a colony, the nation established an independent power; that when, by indulgence and favour, emigrants are become rich, they shall not contribute to their own defence, but at their own pleasure; and that they shall not be included, like millions of their fellow-subjects, in the general system of representation; involves such an accumulation of absurdity, as nothing but the shew of patriotism could palliate.

He that accepts protection, stipulates obedience. We have always protected the Americans; we may therefore subject them to government.

The less is included in the greater. That power which can take away life, may seize upon property. The parliament may enact for America a law of capital punishment; it may therefore establish a mode and proportion of taxation.

But there are some who lament the state of the poor Bostonians, because they cannot all be supposed to have committed acts of rebellion, yet all are involved in the penalty imposed. This, they say, is to violate the first rule of justice, by condemning the innocent to suffer with the guilty.

This deserves some notice, as it seems dictated by equity and humanity, however it may raise contempt, by the ignorance which it betrays of the state of man, and the system of things. That the innocent should be confounded with the guilty, is undoubtedly an evil; but it is an evil which no care or caution can prevent. National crimes require national punishments, of which many must necessarily have their part, who have not incurred them by personal guilt. If rebels should fortify a town, the cannon of lawful authority will endanger equally the harmless burghers and the criminal garrison.

In some cases, those suffer most who are least intended to be hurt. If the French in the late war had taken an English city, and permitted the natives to keep their dwellings, how could it have been recovered, but by the slaughter of our friends? A bomb might as well destroy an Englishman as a Frenchman; and by famine we know that the inhabitants would be the first that should perish.

This infliction of promiscuous evil may therefore be lamented, but cannot be blamed. The power of lawful government must be maintained; and the miseries which rebellion produces, can be charged only on the rebels.

That man likewise is *not a Patriot*, who denies his governors their due praise, and who conceals from the people the benefits which they receive. Those therefore can lay no claim to this illustrious appellation, who impute want of public spirit to the late parliament; an assembly of men, whom, notwithstanding some fluctuation of counsel, and some weakness of agency, the nation must always remember with gratitude, since it is indebted to them for a very ample concession in the resignation of protections, and a wise and honest attempt to improve the constitution, in the new judicature instituted for the trial of elections.

The right of protection, which might be necessary when it was first claimed, and was very consistent with that liberality of immunities in which the feudal constitution delighted, was by its nature liable to abuse, and had in reality been sometimes misapplied, to the evasion of the law and the defeat of justice. The evil was perhaps not adequate to the clamour; nor is it very certain, that the possible good of this privilege was not more than

The Patriot

equal to the possible evil. It is however plain, that whether they gave any thing or not to the Public, they at least lost something from themselves. They divested their dignity of a very splendid distinction, and shewed that they were more willing than their predecessors to stand on a level with their fellow subjects.

The new mode of trying elections, if it be found effectual, will diffuse its consequences further than seems yet to be foreseen. It is, I believe, generally considered as advantageous only to those who claim seats in parliament; but, if to chuse representatives be one of the most valuable rights of Englishmen, every voter must consider that law as adding to his happiness, which makes his suffrage efficacious; since it was vain to chuse, while the election could be controlled by any other power.

With what imperious contempt of ancient rights, and what audaciousness of arbitrary authority, former parliaments have judged the disputes about elections, it is not necessary to relate. The claim of a candidate, and the right of electors are said scarcely to have been, even in appearance, referred to conscience; but to have been decided by party, by passion, by prejudice, or by frolic. To have friends in the borough was of little use to him, who wanted friends in the house; a pretence was easily found to evade a majority, and the seat was at last his, that was chosen not by his electors, but his fellow-senators.

Thus the nation was insulted with a mock election, and the parliament was filled with spurious representatives; one of the most important claims, that of a right to sit in the supreme council of the kingdom, was debated in jest, and no man could be confident of success from the justice of his cause.

A disputed election is now tried with the same scrupulousness and solemnity, as any other title. The candidate that has deserved well of his neighbours, may now be certain of enjoying the effect of their approbation; and the elector, who has voted honestly for known merit, may be certain that he has not voted in vain.

Such was the parliament, which some of those, who are now aspiring to sit in another, have taught the rabble to consider as an unlawful convention of men, worthless, venal, and prostitute, slaves of the court, and tyrants of the people.

That the next House of Commons may act upon the principles of the last, with more constancy and higher spirit, must be the

The Patriot

wish of all who wish well to the Publick; and it is surely not too much to expect, that the nation will recover from its delusion, and unite in a general abhorrence of those who, by deceiving the credulous with fictitious mischiefs, overbearing the weak by audacity of falsehood, by appealing to the judgment of ignorance, and flattering the vanity of meanness, by slandering honesty and insulting dignity, have gathered round them whatever the kingdom can supply of base, and gross, and profligate; and *raised by merit to this bad eminence*, arrogate to themselves the name of PATRIOTS.

8
Taxation No Tyranny
(1775)

In all the parts of human knowledge, whether terminating in science merely speculative, or operating upon life private or civil, are admitted some fundamental principles, or common axioms, which being generally received are little doubted, and being little doubted have been rarely proved.

Of these gratuitous and acknowledged truths it is often the fate to become less evident by endeavours to explain them, however necessary such endeavours may be made by the misapprehensions of absurdity, or the sophistries of interest. It is difficult to prove the principles of science, because notions cannot always be found more intelligible than those which are questioned. It is difficult to prove the principles of practice, because they have for the most part not been discovered by investigation, but obtruded by experience, and the demonstrator will find, after an operose deduction, that he has been trying to make that seen which can be only felt.

Of this kind is the position, that *the supreme power of every community has the right of requiring from all its subjects such contributions as are necessary to the public safety or public prosperity*, which was considered by all mankind as comprising the primary and essential condition of all political society, till it became disputed by those zealots of anarchy, who have denied to the Parliament of Britain the right of taxing the American Colonies.

In favour of this exemption of the Americans from the authority of their lawful sovereign, and the dominion of their mother-country, very loud clamours have been raised, and many wild assertions advanced, which by such as borrow their opinions from the reigning fashion have been admitted as arguments; and what is strange, though their tendency is to lessen English honour, and English power, have been heard by English-men with a wish to find them true. Passion has in its first violence controlled interest, as the eddy for a while runs against the stream.

To be prejudiced is always to be weak; yet there are prejudices so near to laudable, that they have been often praised, and are always pardoned. To love their country has been considered as virtue in men, whose love could not be otherwise than blind, because their preference was made without a comparison; but it has never been my fortune to find, either in ancient or modern writers, any honourable mention of those, who have with equal blindness hated their country.

These antipatriotic prejudices are the abortions of Folly impregnated by Faction, which being produced against the standing order of Nature, have not strength sufficient for long life. They are born only to scream and perish, and leave those to contempt or detestation, whose kindness was employed to nurse them into mischief.

To perplex the opinion of the Publick many artifices have been used, which, as usually happens when falsehood is to be maintained by fraud, lose their force by counteracting one another.

The nation is sometimes to be mollified by a tender tale of men, who fled from tyranny to rocks and deserts, and is persuaded to lose all claims of justice, and all sense of dignity, in compassion for a harmless people, who having worked hard for bread in a wild country, and obtained by the slow progression of manual industry the accommodations of life, are now invaded by unprecedented oppression, and plundered of their properties by the harpies of taxation.

We are told how their industry is obstructed by unnatural restraints, and their trade confined by rigorous prohibitions; how they are forbidden to enjoy the products of their own soil, to manufacture the materials which Nature spreads before them, or to carry their own goods to the nearest market: and surely the generosity of English virtue will never heap new weight upon those that are already overladen, will never delight in that dominion, which cannot be exercised but by cruelty and outrage.

But while we are melting in silent sorrow, and in the transports of delirious pity dropping both the sword and balance from our

Taxation No Tyranny

hands, another friend of the Americans thinks it better to awaken another passion, and tries to alarm our interest, or excite our veneration, by accounts of their greatness and their opulence, of the fertility of their land, and the splendour of their towns. We then begin to consider the question with more evenness of mind, are ready to conclude that those restrictions are not very oppressive which have been found consistent with this speedy growth of prosperity, and begin to think it reasonable that they, who thus flourish under the protection of our government, should contribute something towards its expence.

But we are soon told that the Americans, however wealthy, cannot be taxed; that they are the descendants of men who left all for liberty, and that they have constantly preserved the principles and stubbornness of their progenitors; that they are too obstinate for persuasion, and too powerful for constraint; that they will laugh at argument, and defeat violence; that the continent of North America contains three millions, not of men merely, but of Whigs, of Whigs fierce for liberty, and disdainful of dominion; that they multiply with the fecundity of their own rattle-snakes, so that every quarter of a century doubles their numbers.

Men accustomed to think themselves masters do not love to be threatened. This talk is, I hope, commonly thrown away, or raises passions different from those which it was intended to excite. Instead of terrifying the English hearer to tame acquiescence, it disposes him to hasten the experiment of bending obstinacy before it is become yet more obdurate, and convinces him that it is necessary to attack a nation thus prolific while we may yet hope to prevail. When he is told through what extent of territory we must travel to subdue them, he recollects how far, a few years ago, we travelled in their defence. When it is urged that they will shoot up like the Hydra, he naturally considers how the Hydra was destroyed.

Nothing dejects a trader like the interruption of his profits. A commercial people, however magnanimous, shrinks at the thought of declining traffick, and an unfavourable balance. The effect of this terrour has been tried. We have been stunned with the importance of our American commerce, and heard of merchants with warehouses that are never to be emptied, and of manufacturers starving for want of work.

Taxation No Tyranny

That our commerce with America is profitable, however less than ostentatious or deceitful estimates have made it, and that it is our interest to preserve it, has never been denied; but surely it will most effectually be preserved, by being kept always in our own power. Concessions may promote it for a moment, but superiority only can ensure its continuance. There will always be a part, and always a very large part of every community that have no care but for themselves, and whose care for themselves reaches little farther than impatience of immediate pain, and eagerness for the nearest good. The blind are said to feel with peculiar nicety. They who look but little into futurity, have perhaps the quickest sensation of the present. A merchant's desire is not of glory, but of gain; not of publick wealth, but of private emolument; he is therefore rarely to be consulted about war and peace, or any designs of wide extent and distant consequence.

Yet this, like other general characters, will sometimes fail. The traders of *Birmingham* have rescued themselves from all imputation of narrow selfishness by a manly recommendation to Parliament of the rights and dignity of their native country.

To these men I do not intend to ascribe an absurd and enthusiastick contempt of interest, but to give them the rational and just praise of distinguishing real from seeming good, of being able to see through the cloud of interposing difficulties, to the lasting and solid happiness of victory and settlement.

Lest all these topicks of persuasion should fail, the great actor of patriotism has tried another, in which terrour and pity are happily combined, not without a proper superaddition of that admiration which latter ages have brought into the drama. The heroes of Boston he tells us, if the stamp act had not been repealed, would have left their town, their port, and their trade, have resigned the splendour of opulence, and quitted the delights of neighbourhood, to disperse themselves over the country, where they would till the ground, and fish in the rivers, and range the mountains, AND BE FREE.

These surely are brave words. If the mere sound of freedom can operate thus powerfully, let no man hereafter doubt the story of the Pied Piper. *The removal of the people of Boston into the country,* seems even to the congress not only *difficult in its execution,* but *important in its consequences.* The difficulty of execution is best known to the Bostonians themselves; the consequence, alas! will only be, that they will leave good houses to wiser men.

Yet before they quit the comforts of a warm home for the sounding something which they think better, he cannot be thought their enemy who advises them to consider well whether they shall find it. By turning fishermen or hunters, woodmen or shepherds they may become wild, but it is not so easy to conceive them free; for who can be more a slave than he that is driven by force from the comforts of life, is compelled to leave his house to a casual comer, and whatever he does, or wherever he wanders, finds every moment some new testimony of his own subjection? If choice of evil be freedom, the felon in the gallies has his option of labour or of stripes. The Bostonian may quit his house to starve in the fields; his dog may refuse to set, and smart under the lash, and they may then congratulate each other upon the smiles of liberty, *profuse of bliss, and pregnant with delight.*

To treat such designs as serious, would be to think too contemptuously of Bostonian understandings. The artifice indeed is not new: the blusterer who threatened in vain to destroy his opponent, has sometimes obtained his end, by making it believe that he would hang himself.

But terrours and pity are not the only means by which the taxation of the Americans is opposed. There are those who profess to use them only as auxiliaries to reason and justice, who tell us, that to tax the Colonies is usurpation and oppression, an invasion of natural and legal rights, and a violation of those principles which support the constitution of English government.

This question is of great importance. That the Americans are able to bear taxation is indubitable; that their refusal may be overruled is highly probable: but power is no sufficient evidence of truth. Let us examine our own claim, and the objections of the recusants, with caution proportioned to the event of the decision, which must convict one part of robbery, or the other of rebellion.

A tax is a payment exacted by authority from part of the community for the benefit of the whole. From whom, and in what proportion such payment shall be required, and to what uses it shall be applied, those only are to judge to whom government is intrusted. In the British dominion taxes are apportioned, levied, and appropriated by the states assembled in parliament.

Taxation No Tyranny

Of every empire all the subordinate communities are liable to taxation, because they all share the benefits of government, and therefore ought all to furnish their proportion of the expence.

This the Americans have never openly denied. That it is their duty to pay the cost of their own safety they seem to admit; nor do they refuse their contribution to the exigencies, whatever they may be, of the British empire; but they make this participation of the public burden a duty of very uncertain extent, and imperfect obligation, a duty temporary, occasional, and elective, of which they reserve to themselves the right of settling the degree, the time, and the duration, of judging when it may be required, and when it has been performed.

They allow to the supreme power nothing more than the liberty of notifying to them its demands or its necessities. Of this notification they profess to think for themselves, how far it shall influence their counsels, and of the necessities alleged, how far they shall endeavour to relieve them. They assume the exclusive power of settling not only the mode, but the quantity of this payment. They are ready to co-operate with all the other dominions of the king; but they will co-operate by no means which they do not like, and at no greater charge than they are willing to bear.

This claim, wild as it may seem, this claim, which supposes dominion without authority, and subjects without subordination, has found among the libertines of policy many clamorous and hardy vindicators. The laws of Nature, the rights of humanity, the faith of charters, the danger of liberty, the encroachments of usurpation, have been thundered in our ears, sometimes by interested faction, and sometimes by honest stupidity.

It is said by Fontenelle, that if twenty philosophers shall resolutely deny that the presence of the sun makes the day, he will not despair but whole nations may adopt the opinion. So many political dogmatists have denied to the Mother-country the power of taxing the Colonies, and have enforced their denial with so much violence of outcry, that their sect is already very numerous, and the publick voice suspends its decision.

In moral and political questions the contest between interest and justice has been often tedious and often fierce, but perhaps it never happened before, that justice found much opposition with interest on her side.

Taxation No Tyranny

For the satisfaction of this inquiry, it is necessary to consider how a Colony is constituted, what are the terms of migration as dictated by Nature, or settled by compact, and what social or political rights the man loses, or acquires, that leaves his country to establish himself in a distant plantation.

Of two modes of migration the history of mankind informs us, and so far as I can yet discover, of two only.

In countries where life was yet unadjusted, and policy unformed, it sometimes happened that by the dissensions of heads of families, by the ambition of daring adventurers, by some accidental pressure of distress, or by the mere discontent of idleness, one part of the community broke off from the rest, and numbers, greater or smaller, forsook their habitations, put themselves under the command of some favourite of fortune, and with or without the consent of their countrymen or governours, went out to see what better regions they could occupy, and in what place, by conquest or by treaty, they could gain a habitation.

Sons of enterprise like these, who committed to their own swords their hopes and their lives, when they left their country, became another nation, with designs and prospects, and interests, of their own. They looked back no more to their former home; they expected no help from those whom they had left behind; if they conquered, they conquered for themselves; if they were destroyed, they were not by any other power either lamented or revenged.

Of this kind seem to have been all the migrations of the early world, whether historical or fabulous, and of this kind were the eruptions of those nations which from the North invaded the Roman empire, and filled Europe with new sovereignties.

But when, by the gradual admission of wiser laws and gentler manners, society became more compacted and better regulated, it was found that the power of every people consisted in union, produced by one common interest, and operating in joint efforts and consistent councils.

From this time Independence perceptibly wasted away. No part of the nation was permitted to act for itself. All now had the same enemies and the same friends; the Government protected individuals, and individuals were required to refer their designs to the prosperity of the Government.

Taxation No Tyranny

By this principle it is, that states are formed and consolidated. Every man is taught to consider his own happiness as combined with the public prosperity, and to think himself great and powerful, in proportion to the greatness and power of his Governors.

Had the Western continent been discovered between the fourth and tenth century, when all the Northern world was in motion; and had navigation been at that time sufficiently advanced to make so long a passage easily practicable, there is little reason for doubting but the intumescence of nations would have found its vent, like all other expansive violence, where there was least resistance; and that Huns and Vandals, instead of fighting their way to the South of Europe, would have gone by thousands and by myriads under their several chiefs to take possession of regions smiling with pleasure and waving with fertility, from which the naked inhabitants were unable to repel them.

Every expedition would in those days of laxity have produced a distinct and independent state. The Scandinavian heroes might have divided the country among them, and have spread the feudal subdivision of regality from Hudson's Bay to the Pacific Ocean.

But Columbus came five or six hundred years too late for the candidates of sovereignty. When he formed his project of discovery, the fluctuations of military turbulence had subsided, and Europe began to regain a settled form, by established government and regular subordination. No man could any longer erect himself into a chieftain, and lead out his fellow-subjects by his own authority to plunder or to war. He that committed any act of hostility by land or sea, without the commission of some acknowledged sovereign, was considered by all mankind as a robber or a pirate, names which were now of little credit, and of which therefore no man was ambitious.

Columbus in a remoter time would have found his way to some discontented Lord, or some younger brother of a petty Sovereign, who would have taken fire at his proposal, and have quickly kindled with equal heat a troop of followers; they would have built ships, or have seized them, and have wandered with him at all adventures as far as they could keep hope in their company. But the age being now past of vagrant excursion and fortuitous hostility, he was under the necessity of travelling from court to court, scorned and repulsed as a wild projector, an idle promiser of

Taxation No Tyranny

kingdoms in the clouds: nor has any part of the world yet had reason to rejoice that he found at last reception and employment.

In the same year, in a year hitherto disastrous to mankind, by the Portuguese was discovered the passage of the Indies, and by the Spaniards the coast of America. The nations of Europe were fired with boundless expectation, and the discoverers pursuing their enterprise, made conquests in both hemispheres of wide extent. But the adventurers were contented with plunder; though they took gold and silver to themselves, they seized islands and kingdoms in the name of their Sovereigns. When a new region was gained, a governour was appointed by that power which had given the commission to the conqueror; nor have I met with any European but Stukeley of London, that formed a design of exalting himself in the newly found countries to independent dominion.

To secure a conquest, it was always necessary to plant a colony, and territories thus occupied and settled were rightly considered as mere extensions or processes of empire; as ramifications which by the circulation of one publick interest communicated with the original source of dominion, and which were kept flourishing and spreading by the radical vigour of the Mother-country.

The Colonies of England differ no otherwise from those of other nations, than as the English constitution differs from theirs. All Government is ultimately and essentially absolute, but subordinate societies may have more immunities, or individuals greater liberty, as the operations of Government are differently conducted. An Englishman in the common course of life and action feels no restraint. An English Colony has very liberal powers of regulating its own manners and adjusting its own affairs. But an English individual may by the supreme authority be deprived of liberty, and a Colony divested of its powers, for reasons of which that authority is the only judge.

In sovereignty there are no gradations. There may be limited royalty, there may be limited consulship; but there can be no limited government. There must in every society be some power or other from which there is no appeal, which admits no restrictions, which pervades the whole mass of the community, regulates and adjusts all subordination, enacts laws or repeals them, erects or annuls judicatures, extends or contracts privileges, exempt itself from question or control, and bounded only by physical necessity.

By this power, wherever it subsists, all legislation and jurisdiction is animated and maintained. From this all legal rights are emanations, which, whether equitably or not, may be legally recalled. It is not infallible, for it may do wrong; but it is irresistible, for it can be resisted only by rebellion, by an act which makes it questionable what shall be thenceforward the supreme power.

An English Colony is a number of persons, to whom the King grants a Charter permitting them to settle in some distant country, and enabling them to constitute a Corporation, enjoying such powers as the Charter grants, to be administered in such forms as the Charter prescribes. As a Corporation they make laws for themselves, but as a Corporation subsisting by a grant from higher authority, to the control of that authority they continue subject.

As men are placed at a greater distance from the Supreme Council of the kingdom, they must be intrusted with ampler liberty of regulating their conduct by their own wisdom. As they are more secluded from easy recourse to national judicature, they must be more extensively commissioned to pass judgment on each other.

For this reason our more important and opulent Colonies see the appearance and feel the effect of a regular Legislature, which in some places has acted so long with unquestioned authority, that it has forgotten whence that authority was originally derived.

To their Charters the Colonies owe, like other corporations, their political existence. The solemnities of legislation, the administration of justice, the security of property, are all bestowed upon them by the royal grant. Without their Charter there would be no power among them, by which any law could be made, or duties enjoined, and debt recovered, or criminal punished.

A Charter is a grant of certain powers or privileges given to a part of the community for the advantage of the whole, and is therefore liable by its nature to change or to revocation. Every act of Government aims at publick good. A Charter, which experience has shewn to be detrimental to the nation, is to be repealed; because general prosperity must always be preferred to particular interest. If a Charter be used to evil purposes, it is forfeited, as the weapon is taken away which is injuriously employed.

Taxation No Tyranny

The Charter therefore by which provincial governments are constituted, may be always legally, and where it is either inconvenient in its nature, or misapplied in its use, may be equitably repealed; by such repeal the whole fabrick of subordination is immediately destroyed, and the constitution sunk at once into a chaos: the society is dissolved into a tumult of individuals, without authority to command, or obligation to obey; without any punishment of wrongs but by personal resentment, or any protection of right but by the hand of the possessor.

A Colony is to the Mother-country as a member to the body, deriving its action and its strength from the general principle of vitality; receiving from the body, and communicating to it, all the benefits and evils of health and disease; liable in dangerous maladies to sharp applications, of which the body however must partake the pain; and exposed, if incurably tainted, to amputation, by which the body likewise will be mutilated.

The Mother-country always considers the Colonies thus connected, as parts of itself; the prosperity or unhappiness of either is the prosperity or unhappiness of both; not perhaps of both in the same degree, for the body may subsist, though less commodiously, without a limb, but the limb must perish if it be parted from the body.

Our Colonies therefore, however distant, have been hitherto treated as constituent parts of the British Empire. The inhabitants incorporated by English Charters, are entitled to all the rights of Englishmen. They are governed by English laws, entitled to English dignities, regulated by English counsels, and protected by English arms; and it seems to follow by consequence not easily avoided, that they are subject to English government, and chargeable by English taxation.

To him that considers the nature, the original, the progress, and the constitution of the Colonies, who remembers that the first discoverers had commissions from the Crown, that the first settlers owe to a Charter their civil forms and regular magistracy, and that all personal immunities and legal securities, by which the condition of the subject has been from time to time improved, have been extended to the Colonists, it will not be doubted but the Parliament of England has a right to bind them by statutes, and *to bind them in all cases whatsoever*, and has therefore a natural and constitutional power of laying upon them any tax or impost, whether external or internal, upon the product of land, or the manufactures of industry, in the exigencies of war, or in the time of profound peace, for the defence of America, *for the purpose of raising a revenue,* or for any other end beneficial to the Empire.

There are some, and those not inconsiderable for number, nor contemptible for knowledge, who except the power of taxation from the general dominion of Parliament, and hold, that whatever degrees of obedience may be exacted, or whatever authority may be exercised in other acts of Government, there is still reverence to be paid to money, and that legislation passes its limits when it violates the purse.

Of this exception, which by a head not fully impregnated with politicks is not easily comprehended, it is alleged as an unanswerable reason, that the Colonies send no representatives to the House of Commons.

It is, say the American advocates, the natural distinction of a freeman, and the legal privilege of an Englishman, that he is able to call his possessions his own, that he can sit secure in the enjoyment of inheritance or acquisition, that his house is fortified by the law, and that nothing can be taken from him but by his own consent. This consent is given for every man by his representative in parliament. The Americans unrepresented cannot consent to English taxations, as a corporation, and they will not consent as individuals.

Of this argument, it has been observed by more than one, that its force extends equally to all other laws, for a freeman is not to be exposed to punishment, or be called to any onerous service but by his own consent. The Congress has extracted a position from the fanciful *Montesquieu,* that *in a free state every man being a free agent ought to be concerned in his own government.* Whatever is true of taxation is true of every other law, that he who is bound by it, without his consent, is not free, for he is not concerned in his own government.

He that denies the English Parliament the right of taxation, denies it likewise the right of making any other laws civil or criminal, yet this power over the Colonies was never yet disputed by themselves. They have always admitted statutes for the punishment of offences, and for the redress or prevention of inconvenien-

Taxation No Tyranny

cies, and the reception of any law draws after it by a chain which cannot be broken, the unwelcome necessity of submitting to taxation.

That a free man is governed by himself, or by laws to which he has consented, is a position of mighty sound: but every man that utters it, with whatever confidence, and every man that hears it, with whatever acquiescence, if consent be supposed to imply the power of refusal, feels it to be false. We virtually and implicitly allow the institutions of any Government of which we enjoy the benefit, and solicit the protection. In wide extended dominions, though power has been diffused with the most even hand, yet a very small part of the people are either primarily or secondarily consulted in Legislation. The business of the Publick must be done by delegation. The choice of delegates is made by a select number, and those who are not electors stand idle and helpless spectators of the commonweal, *wholly unconcerned in the government of themselves.*

Of Electors the hap is but little better. They are often far from unanimity in their choice, and where the numbers approach to equality, almost half must be governed not only without, but against their choice.

How any man can have consented to institutions established in distant ages, it will be difficult to explain. In the most favourite residence of liberty, the consent of individuals is merely passive, a tacit admission in every community of the terms which that community grants and requires. As all are born the subjects of some state or other, we may be said to have been all born consenting to some system of Government. Other consent than this, the condition of civil life does not allow. It is the unmeaning clamour of the pedants of policy, the delirious dream of republican fanaticism.

But hear, ye sons and daughters of liberty, the sounds which the winds are wafting from the Western Continent. The Americans are telling one another, what, if we may judge from their noisy triumph, they have but lately discovered, and what yet is a very important truth: *That they are entitled to Life, Liberty, and Property, and that they have never ceded to any sovereign power whatever a right to dispose of either without their consent.*

While this resolution stands alone, the Americans are free from singularity of opinion; their wit has not yet betrayed them to

Taxation No Tyranny

heresy. While they speak as the naked sons of Nature, they claim but what is claimed by other men, and have withheld nothing but what all with-hold. They are here upon firm ground, behind entrenchments which never can be forced.

Humanity is very uniform. The Americans have this resemblance to Europeans, that they do not always know when they are well. They soon quit the fortress that could neither have been mined by sophistry, nor battered by declamation. Their next resolution declares, that *their ancestors, who first settled the Colonies, were, at the time of their emigration from the Mother-country, entitled to all the rights, liberties, and immunities of free and natural-born subjects within the realm of England.*

This likewise is true; but when this is granted, their boast of original rights is at an end; they are no longer in a State of Nature. These lords of themselves, these kings of *Me*, these demigods of independence, sink down to Colonists, governed by a Charter. If their ancestors were subjects, they acknowledged a Sovereign; if they had a right to English privileges, they were accountable to English laws, and what must grieve the Lover of Liberty to discover, had ceded to the King and Parliament, whether the right or not, at least the power of disposing, *without their consent, of their lives, liberties, and properties.* It therefore is required of them to prove, that the Parliament ever ceded to them a dispensation from that obedience, which they owe as natural-born subjects, or any degree of independence or immunity not enjoyed by other Englishmen.

They say, That by such emigration they by no means forfeited, surrendered, or lost any of those rights; but that *they were, and their descendants now are, entitled to the exercise and enjoyment of all such of them as their local and other circumstances enable them to exercise and enjoy.*

That they who form a settlement by a lawful Charter having committed no crime forfeit no privileges, will be readily confessed; but what they do not forfeit by any judicial sentence, they may lose by natural effects. As man can be but in one place at once, he cannot have the advantages of multiplied residence. He that will enjoy the brightness of sunshine, must quit the coolness of the shade. He who goes voluntarily to America, cannot complain of losing what he leaves in Europe. He perhaps had a right to vote for a knight or burgess; by crossing the Atlantick he has not nullified

Taxation No Tyranny

his right; but he has made its exertion no longer possible.[1] By his own choice he has left a country where he had a vote and little property, for another, where he has great property, but no vote. But as this preference was deliberate and unconstrained, he is still *concerned in the government of himself*; he has reduced himself from a voter to one of the innumerable multitude that have no vote. He has truly *ceded his right*, but he still is governed by his own consent; because he has consented to throw his atom of interest into the general mass of the community. Of the consequences of his own act he has no cause to complain; he has chosen, or intended to chuse, the greater good; he is represented, as himself desired, in the general representation.

But the privileges of an American scorn the limits of place; they are part of himself, and cannot be lost by departure from his country; they float in the air, or glide under the ocean.

Doris amara suam non intermisceat undam.

A Planter, wherever he settles, is not only a freeman, but a legislator, *ubi imperator, ibi Roma. As the English Colonists are not represented in the British Parliament, they are entitled to a free and exclusive power of legislation in their several legislatures, in all cases of Taxation and internal polity, subject only to the negative of the Sovereign, in such manner as has been heretofore used and accustomed. We cheerfully consent to the operation of such acts of the British Parliament as are* bone fide *restrained to the regulation of our external commerce—excluding every idea of Taxation, internal or external, for raising a revenue on the subjects of America without their consent.*

Their reason for this claim is, *that the foundation of English Liberty, and of all Government, is a right in the People to participate in their Legislative Council.*

They inherit, they say, *from their ancestors, the right which their ancestors possessed, of enjoying all the privileges of Englishmen.* That they inherit the right of their ancestors is allowed; but they can inherit no more. Their ancestors left a country where the representatives of the people were elected by men particularly qualified, and where those who wanted qualifications, or who did not use them, were bound by the decisions of men, whom they had not deputed.

[1] Of this reasoning, I owe part to a conversation with Sir John Hawkins.

Taxation No Tyranny

The colonists are the descendants of men, who either had no vote in elections, or who voluntarily resigned them for something, in their opinion, of more estimation: they have therefore exactly what their ancestors left them, not a vote in making laws, or in constituting legislators, but the happiness of being protected by law, and the duty of obeying it.

What their ancestors did not carry with them, neither they nor their descendants have since acquired. They have not, by abandoning their part in one legislature, obtained the power of constituting another, exclusive and independent, any more than the multitudes, who are now debarred from voting, have a right to erect a separate Parliament for themselves.

Men are wrong for want of sense, but they are wrong by halves for want of spirit. Since the Americans have discovered that they can make a Parliament, whence comes it that they do not think themselves equally empowered to make a King? If they are subjects, whose government is constituted by a Charter, they can form no body of independent legislature. If their rights are inherent and underived, they may by their own suffrages encircle with a diadem the brows of Mr. Cushing.

It is farther declared by the Congress of Philadelphia, *that his Majesty's Colonies are entitled to all the privileges and immunities granted and confirmed to them by Royal Charters, or secured to them by their several codes of provincial laws.*

The first clause of this resolution is easily understood, and will be readily admitted. To all the privileges which a Charter can convey, they are by a Royal Charter evidently entitled. The second clause is of greater difficulty; for how can a provincial law secure privileges or immunities to a province? Provincial laws may grant to certain individuals of the province the enjoyment of gainful, or an immunity from onerous offices; they may operate upon the people to whom they relate; but no province can confer provincial privileges on itself. They may have a right to all which the King has given them; but it is a conceit of the other hemisphere, that men have a right to all which they have given to themselves.

A corporation is considered in law as an individual, and can no more extend its own immunities, than a man can by his own choice assume dignities or titles.

The Legislature of a Colony, let not the comparison be too much

Taxation No Tyranny

disdained, is only the vestry of a larger parish, which may lay a cess on the inhabitants, and enforce the payment; but can extend no influence beyond its own district, must modify its particular regulations by the general law, and whatever may be its internal expences, is still liable to Taxes laid by superior authority.

The Charters given to different provinces are different, and no general right can be extracted from them. The Charter of Pennsylvania, where this Congress of anarchy has been impudently held, contains a clause admitting in express terms Taxation by the Parliament. If in the other Charters no such reserve is made, it must have been omitted as not necessary, because it is implied in the nature of subordinate government. They who are subject to laws, are liable to Taxes. If any such immunity had been granted, it is still revocable by the Legislature, and ought to be revoked, as contrary to the publick good, which is in every Charter ultimately intended.

Suppose it true, that any such exemption is contained in the Charter of Maryland, it can be pleaded only by the Marylanders. It is of no use for any other province, and with regard even to them, must have been considered as one of the grants in which the King has been deceived, and annulled as mischievous to the Publick, by sacrificing to one little settlement the general interest of the Empire; as infringing the system of dominion, and violating the compact of Government. But Dr. Tucker has shewn that even this Charter promises no exemption from Parliamentary Taxes.

In the controversy agitated about the beginning of this century, whether the English laws could bind Ireland, Davenant, who defended against Molyneux the claims of England, considered it as necessary to prove nothing more, than that the present Irish must be deemed a Colony.

The necessary connexion of representatives with Taxes, seems to have sunk deep into many of those minds, that admit sounds without their meaning.

Our nation is represented in Parliament by an assembly as numerous as can well consist with order and dispatch, chosen by persons so differently qualified in different places, that the mode of choice seems to be, for the most part, formed by chance, and settled by custom. Of individuals far the greater part have no vote,

Taxation No Tyranny

and of the voters few have any personal knowledge of him to whom they intrust their liberty and fortune.

Yet this representation has the whole effect expected or desired; that of spreading so wide the care of general interest, and the participation of publick counsels, that the advantage or corruption of particular men can seldom operate with much injury to the Publick.

For this reason many populous and opulent towns neither enjoy nor desire particular representatives: they are included in the general scheme of publick administration, and cannot suffer but with the rest of the Empire.

It is urged that the Americans have not the same security, and that a British Legislator may wanton with their property; yet if it be true, that their wealth is our wealth, and that their ruin will be our ruin, the Parliament has the same interest in attending to them, as to any other part of the nation. The reason why we place any confidence in our representatives is, that they must share in the good or evil which their counsels shall produce. Their share is indeed commonly consequential and remote; but it is not often possible that any immediate advantage can be extended to such numbers as may prevail against it. We are therefore as secure against intentional depravations of Government as human wisdom can make us, and upon this security the Americans may venture to repose.

It is said by the *Old Member* who has written an *Appeal* against the Tax, that *as the produce of American labour is spent in British manufactures, the balance of trade is greatly against them; whatever you take directly in Taxes, is in effect taken from your own commerce. If the minister seizes the money with which the American should pay his debts and come to market, the merchant cannot expect him as a customer, nor can the debts already contracted be paid.—Suppose we obtain from America a million instead of one hundred thousand pounds, it would be supplying one personal exigence by the future ruin of our commerce.*

Part of this is true; but the *Old Member* seems not to perceive, that if his brethren of the Legislature know this as well as himself, the Americans are in no danger of oppression, since by men commonly provident they must be so taxed, as that we may not lose one way what we gain another.

Taxation No Tyranny

The same *Old Member* has discovered, that the judges formerly thought it illegal to tax Ireland, and declares that no cases can be more alike than those of Ireland and America; yet the judges whom he quotes have mentioned a difference. Ireland, they say, *hath a Parliament of its own*. When any Colony has an independent Parliament acknowledged by the Parliament of Britain, the cases will differ less. Yet by the 6 Geo. I. chap. 5. the Acts of the British Parliament bind Ireland.

It is urged that when Wales, Durham, and Chester were divested of their particular privileges or ancient government, and reduced to the state of English counties, they had representatives assigned them.

To those from whom something had been taken, something in return might properly be given. To the Americans their Charters are left as they were, nor have they lost any thing except that of which their sedition has deprived them. If they were to be represented in Parliament, something would be granted, though nothing is withdrawn.

The inhabitants of Chester, Durham, and Wales, were invited to exchange their peculiar institutions for the power of voting, which they wanted before. The Americans have voluntarily resigned the power of voting, to live in distant and separate governments, and what they have voluntarily quitted, they have no right to claim.

It must always be remembered that they are represented by the same virtual representation as the greater part of Englishmen; and that if by change of place they have less share in the Legislature than is proportionate to their opulence, they by their removal gained that opulence, and had originally and have now their choice of a vote at home, or riches at a distance.

We are told, what appears to the *Old Member* and to others a position that must drive us into inextricable absurdity, that we have either no right, or the sole right of taxing the Colonies. The meaning is, that if we can tax them, they cannot tax themselves; and that if they can tax themselves, we cannot tax them. We answer with very little hesitation, that for the general use of the Empire we have the sole right of taxing them. If they have contributed any thing in their own assemblies, what they contributed was not paid, but given; it was not a tax or tribute, but a present. Yet they have

Taxation No Tyranny

the natural and legal power of levying money on themselves for provincial purposes, of providing for their own expence, at their own discretion. Let not this be thought new or strange; it is the state of every parish in the kingdom.

The friends of the Americans are of different opinions. Some think that being unrepresented they ought to tax themselves, and others that they ought to have representatives in the British Parliament.

If they are to tax themselves, what power is to remain in the supreme Legislature? That they must settle their own mode of levying their money is supposed. May the British Parliament tell them how much they shall contribute? If the sum may be prescribed, they will return few thanks for the power of raising it; if they are at liberty to grant or to deny, they are no longer subjects.

If they are to be represented, what number of these western orators are to be admitted? This I suppose the parliament must settle; yet if men have a natural and unalienable right to be represented, who shall determine the number of their delegates? Let us however suppose them to send twenty-three, half as many as the kingdom of Scotland, what will this representation avail them? To pay taxes will be still a grievance. The love of money will not be lessened, nor the power of getting it increased.

Whither will this necessity of representation drive us? Is every petty settlement to be out of the reach of government, till it has sent a senator to Parliament; or may two of them or a greater number be forced to unite in a single deputation? What at last is the difference between him that is taxed by compulsion without representation, and him that is represented by compulsion in order to be taxed?

For many reigns the House of Commons was in a state of fluctuation: new burgesses were added from time to time, without any reason now to be discovered; but the number has been fixed for more than a century and a half, and the king's power of increasing it has been questioned. It will hardly be thought fit to new-model the constitution in favour of the planters, who, as they grow rich, may buy estates in England, and without any innovation, effectually represent their native colonies.

The friends of the Americans indeed ask for them what they do not ask for themselves. This inestimable right of representation

Taxation No Tyranny

they have never solicited. They mean not to exchange solid money for such airy honour. They say, and say willingly, that they cannot conveniently be represented; because their inference is, that they cannot be taxed. They are too remote to share the general government, and therefore claim the privilege of governing themselves.

Of the principles contained in the resolutions of the Congress, however wild, indefinite, and obscure, such has been the influence upon American understanding, that from New-England to South-Carolina there is formed a general combination of all the Provinces against their Mother-country. The madness of independence has spread from Colony to Colony, till order is lost and government despised, and all is filled with misrule, uproar, violence, and confusion. To be quiet is disaffection, to be loyal is treason.

The Congress of Philadelphia, an assembly convened by its own authority, has promulgated a declaration, in compliance with which the communication between Britain and the greatest part of North America is now suspended. They ceased to admit the importation of English goods in December 1774, and determine to permit the exportation of their own no longer than to November 1775.

This might seem enough, but they have done more. They have declared, that they shall treat all as enemies who do not concur with them in disaffection and perverseness, and that they will trade with none that shall trade with Britain.

They threaten to stigmatize in their Gazette those who shall consume the products or merchandise of their Mother-country, and are now searching suspected houses for prohibited goods.

These hostile declarations they profess themselves ready to maintain by force. They have armed the militia of their provinces, and seized the publick stores of ammunition. They are therefore no longer subjects, since they refuse the laws of their Sovereign, and in defence of that refusal are making open preparations for war.

Being now in their own opinion free states, they are not only raising armies, but forming alliances, not only hastening to rebel themselves, but seducing their neighbours to rebellion. They have published an address to the inhabitants of Quebec, in which discontent and resistance are openly incited, and with very respectful mention of *the sagacity of Frenchmen*, invite them to send deputies to the Congress of Philadelphia, to that seat of Virtue and Veracity,

Taxation No Tyranny

whence the people of England are told, that to establish popery, *a religion fraught with sanguinary and impious tenets*, even in Quebec, a country of which the inhabitants are papists, is so contrary to the constitution that it cannot be lawfully done by the legislature itself; where it is made one of the articles of their association, to deprive the conquered French of their religious establishment; and whence the French of Quebec are, at the same time, flattered into sedition, by professions of expecting *from the liberality of sentiment, distinguishing* their *nation,* that *difference of religion will not prejudice them against a hearty amity,* because *the transcendent nature of freedom elevates all who unite in the cause above such low-minded infirmities.*

Quebec, however, is at a great distance. They have aimed a stroke from which they may hope for greater and more speedy mischief. They have tried to infect the people of England with the contagion of disloyalty. Their credit is happily not such as gives them influence proportionate to their malice. When they talk of their pretended immunities *guarrantied by the plighted faith of Government, and the most solemn compacts with English Sovereigns,* we think ourselves at liberty to inquire when the faith was plighted and the compact made; and when we can only find that King James and King Charles the First promised the settlers in Massachuset's Bay, now famous by the appellation of Bostonians, exemption from taxes for seven years, we infer with Mr. Mauduit, that by this *solemn compact*, they were, after expiration of the stipulated term, liable to taxation.

When they apply to our compassion, by telling us, that they are to be carried from their own country to be tried for certain offences, we are not so ready to pity them, as to advise them not to offend. While they are innocent they are safe.

When they tell of laws made expressly for their punishment, we answer, that tumults and sedition were always punishable, and that the new law prescribes only the mode of execution.

When it is said that the whole town of Boston is distressed for a misdemeanour of a few, we wonder at their shamefulness; for we know that the town of Boston, and all the associated provinces, are now in rebellion to defend or justify the criminals.

If frauds in the imposts of Boston are tried by commission without a jury, they are tried here in the same mode; and why should

Taxation No Tyranny

the Bostonians expect from us more tenderness for them than for ourselves?

If they are condemned unheard, it is because there is no need of a trial. The crime is manifest and notorious. All trial is the investigation of something doubtful. An Italian philosopher observes, that no man desires to hear what he has already seen.

If their assemblies have been suddenly dissolved, what was the reason? Their deliberations were indecent, and their intentions seditious. The power of dissolution is granted and reserved for such times of turbulence. Their best friends have been lately soliciting the King to dissolve his Parliament, to do what they so loudly complain of suffering.

That the same vengeance involves the innocent and guilty is an evil to be lamented, but human caution cannot prevent it, nor human power always redress it. To bring misery on those who have not deserved it, is part of the aggregated guilt of rebellion.

That governours have been sometimes given them only that a great man might get ease from importunity, and that they have judges not always of the deepest learning, or the purest integrity, we have no great reason to doubt, because such misfortunes happen to ourselves. Whoever is governed will sometimes be governed ill, even when he is most *concerned in his own government*.

That improper officers or magistrates are sent, is the crime or folly of those that sent them. When incapacity is discovered, it ought to be removed; if corruption is detected, it ought to be punished. No government could subsist for a day, if single errors could justify defection.

One of their complaints is not such as can claim much commiseration from the softest bosom. They tell us, that we have changed our conduct, and that a tax is now laid by Parliament on those which were never taxed by Parliament before. To this we think it may be easily answered, that the longer they have been spared, the better they can pay.

It is certainly not much their interest to represent innovation as criminal or invidious; for they have introduced into the history of mankind a new mode of disaffection, and have given, I believe, the first example of a proscription published by a Colony against the Mother-country.

To what is urged of new powers granted to the Courts of Ad-

Taxation No Tyranny

miralty, or the extension of authority conferred on the judges, it may be answered in a few words, that they have themselves made such regulations necessary; that they are established for the prevention of greater evils; at the same time, it must be observed, that these powers have not been extended since the rebellion in America.

One mode of persuasion their ingenuity has suggested, which it may perhaps be less easy to resist. That we may not look with indifference on the American contest, or imagine that the struggle is for a claim, which, however decided, is of small importance and remote consequence, the Philadelphian Congress has taken care to inform us, that they are resisting the demands of Parliament, as well for our sakes as their own.

Their keenness of perspicacity has enabled them to pursue consequences to a great distance; to see through clouds impervious to the dimness of European sight; and to find, I know not how, that when they are taxed, we shall be enslaved.

That slavery is a miserable state we have been often told, and doubtless many a Briton will tremble to find it so near as in America; but how it will be brought hither, the Congress must inform us. The question might distress a common understanding; but the statesmen of the other hemisphere can easily resolve it. Our ministers, they say, are our enemies, and *if they should carry the point of taxation, may with the same army enslave us. It may be said, we will not pay them;* but remember, say the western sages, *the taxes from America, and we may add the men, and particularly the Roman Catholics of this vast continent will then be in the power of your enemies. Nor have you any reason to expect, that after making slaves of us, many of us will refuse to assist in reducing you to the same abject state.*

These are dreadful menaces; but suspecting that they have not much the sound of probability, the Congress proceeds: *Do not treat this as chimerical. Know that in less than half a century the quit-rents reserved to the crown from the numberless grants of this vast continent will pour large streams of wealth into the royal coffers. If to this be added the power of taxing America at pleasure, the crown will possess more treasure than may be necessary to purchase* the remains *of liberty in your island.*

All this is very dreadful; but amidst the terror that shakes my frame, I cannot forbear to wish that some sluice were opened for

Taxation No Tyranny

these streams of treasure. I should gladly see America return half of what England has expended in her defence; and of the stream that will *flow so largely in less than half a century*, I hope a small rill at least may be found to quench the thirst of the present generation, which seems to think itself in more danger of wanting money than of losing liberty.

It is difficult to judge with what intention such airy bursts of malevolence are vented: if such writers hope to deceive, let us rather repel them with scorn, than refute them by disputation.

In this last terrifick paragraph are two positions that, if our fears do not overpower our reflection, may enable us to support life a little longer. We are told by these croakers of calamity, not only that our present ministers design to enslave us, but that the same malignity of purpose is to descend through all their successors, and that the wealth to be poured into England by the Pactolus of America will, whenever it comes, be employed to purchase *the remains of liberty*.

Of those who now conduct the national affairs we may, without much arrogance, presume to know more than themselves, and of those who shall succeed them, whether minister or king, not to know less.

The other position is, that the *Crown*, if this laudable opposition should not be successful, *will have the power of taxing America at pleasure*. Surely they think rather too meanly of our apprehensions, when they suppose us not to know what they well know themselves, that they are taxed, like all other British subjects, by Parliament; and that the Crown has not by the new imposts, whether right or wrong, obtained any additional power over their possessions.

It were a curious, but an idle speculation to inquire, what effect these dictators of sedition expect from the dispersion of their letter among us. If they believe their own complaints of hardship, and really dread the danger which they describe, they will naturally hope to communicate the same perceptions to their fellow-subjects. But probably in America, as in other places, the chiefs are incendiaries, that hope to rob in the tumults of a conflagration, and toss brands among a rabble passively combustible. Those who wrote the Address, though they have shown no great extent or profundity of mind, are yet probably wiser than to believe it: but they have been taught by some master of mischief, how to put in motion

Taxation No Tyranny

the engine of political electricity; to attract by the sounds of Liberty and Property, to repel by those of Popery and Slavery; and to give the great stroke by the name of Boston.

When subordinate communities oppose the decrees of the general legislature with defiance thus audacious, and malignity thus acrimonious, nothing remains but to conquer or to yield; to allow their claim of independence, or to reduce them by force to submission and allegiance.

It might be hoped, that no Englishman could be found, whom the menaces of our own Colonists, just rescued from the French, would not move to indignation, like that of the Scythians, who, returning from war, found themselves excluded from their own houses by their slaves.

That corporations constituted by favour, and existing by sufferance, should dare to prohibit commerce with their native country, and threaten individuals by infamy, and societies with at least suspension of amity, for daring to be more obedient to government than themselves, is a degree of insolence, which not only deserves to be punished, but of which the punishment is loudly demanded by the order of life, and the peace of nations.

Yet there have risen up, in the face of the publick, men who, by whatever corruptions or whatever infatuation, have undertaken to defend the Americans, endeavour to shelter them from resentment, and propose reconciliation without submission.

As political diseases are naturally contagious, let it be supposed for a moment that Cornwall, seized with the Philadelphian frenzy, may resolve to separate itself from the general system of the English constitution, and judge of its own rights in its own parliament. A Congress might then meet at Truro, and address the other counties in a style not unlike the language of the American patriots.

"Friends and Fellow-subjects,
We the delegates of the several towns and parishes of Cornwall, assembled to deliberate upon our own state and that of our constituents, having, after serious debate and calm consideration, settled the scheme of our future conduct, hold it necessary to declare the resolutions which we think ourselves entitled to form by the unalienable rights of reasonable Beings, and into which we have been compelled by grievances and oppressions, long endured by us in patient silence, not because we did not

Taxation No Tyranny

feel, or could not remove them, but because we were unwilling to give disturbance to a settled government, and hoped that others would in time find like ourselves their true interest and their original powers, and all co-operate to universal happiness. But since having long indulged the pleasing expectation, we find general discontent not likely to increase, or not likely to end in general defection, we resolve to erect alone the standard of liberty.

Know then, that you are no longer to consider Cornwall as an English county, visited by English judges, receiving law from an English Parliament, or included in any general taxation of the kingdom; but as a state distinct, and independent, governed by its own institutions, administered by its own magistrates, and exempt from any tax or tribute but such as we shall impose upon ourselves.

We are the acknowledged descendants of the earliest inhabitants of Britain, of men, who before the time of history took possession of the island desolate and waste, and therefore open to the first occupants. Of this descent, our language is a sufficient proof, which, not quite a century ago, was different from yours.

Such are the Cornishmen; but who are you? who but the unauthorised and lawless children of intruders, invaders, and oppressors? who but the transmitters of wrong, the inheritors of robbery? In claiming independence we claim but little. We might require you to depart from a land which you possess by usurpation, and to restore all that you have taken from us.

Independence is the gift of Nature. No man is born the master of another. Every Cornishman is a freeman, for we have never resigned the rights of humanity; and he only can be thought free, who is not governed but by his own consent.

You may urge that the present system of government has descended through many ages, and that we have a larger part in the representation of the kingdom, than any other county.

All this is true, but it is neither cogent nor persuasive. We look to the original of things. Our union with the English counties was either compelled by force, or settled by compact.

That which was made by violence, may by violence be broken. If we were treated as a conquered people, our rights might be obscured, but could never be extinguished. The sword can give nothing but power, which a sharper sword can take away.

If our union was by compact, whom could the compact bind but those that concurred in the stipulations? We gave our ancestors no commission to settle the terms of future existence. They might be cowards that were frighted, or blockheads that were cheated; but whatever they were, they could contract only for themselves. What they could establish, we can annul.

Against our present form of government it shall stand in the place of all argument, that we do not like it. While we are governed as we do not like, where is our liberty? We do not like taxes, we will therefore not be taxed, we do not like your laws, and will not obey them.

The taxes laid by our representatives are laid, you tell us, by our own consent: but we will no longer consent to be represented. Our number of legislators was originally a burden, and ought to have been refused: it is now considered as a disproportionate advantage; who then will complain we resign it?

We shall form a Senate of our own, under a President whom the King shall nominate, but whose authority we will limit, by adjusting his salary to his merit. We will not with-hold a proper share of contribution to the necessary expence of lawful government, but we will decide for ourselves what share is proper, what expence is necessary, and what government is lawful.

Till our counsel is proclaimed independent and unaccountable, we will, after the tenth day of September, keep our Tin in our own hands: you can be supplied from no other place, and must therefore comply or be poisoned with the copper of your own kitchens.

If any Cornishman shall refuse his name to this just and laudable association, he shall be tumbled from St. Michael's Mount, or buried alive in a tin-mine; and if any emissary shall be found seducing Cornishmen to their former state, he shall be smeared with tar, and rolled in feathers, and chased with dogs out of our dominions.

From the Cornish Congress at Truro."

Of this memorial what could be said but that it was written in jest, or written by a madman? Yet I know not whether the warmest admirers of Pennsylvanian eloquence can find any argument in the Addresses of the Congress, that is not with greater strength urged by the Cornishman.

The argument of the irregular troops of controversy, stripped of its colours, and turned out naked to the view, is no more than this. Liberty is the birthright of man, and where obedience is compelled, there is no Liberty. The answer is equally simple. Government is necessary to man, and where obedience is not compelled, there is no government.

If the subject refuses to obey, it is the duty of authority to use compulsion. Society cannot subsist but by the power, first of making laws, and then of enforcing them.

To one of the threats hissed out by the Congress, I have put nothing similar into the Cornish proclamation; because it is too wild for folly and too foolish for madness. If we do not withhold our King and his Parliament from taxing them, they will cross the Atlantick and enslave us.

How they will come they have not told us; perhaps they will take wing, and light upon our coasts. When the cranes thus begin to flutter, it is time for pygmies to keep their eyes about them. The Great Orator observes, that they will be very fit, after they have been taxed, to impose chains upon us. If they are so fit as their friend describes them, and so willing as they describe themselves, let us increase our army, and double our militia.

It has been of late a very general practice to talk of slavery among those who are setting at defiance every power that keeps the world in order. If the learned author of the *Reflections on Learning* has rightly observed, that no man ever could give law to language, it will be vain to prohibit the use of the word *slavery*; but I could wish it more discreetly uttered; it is driven at one time too hard into our ears by the loud hurricane of Pennsylvanian eloquence, and at another glides too cold into our hearts by the soft conveyance of a female patriot bewailing the miseries of her *friends and fellow-citizens*.

Such has been the progress of sedition, that those who a few years ago disputed only our right of laying taxes, now question the validity of every act of legislation. They consider themselves as emancipated from obedience, and as being no longer the subjects of the British Crown. They leave us no choice but of yielding or conquering, of resigning our dominion, or maintaining it by force.

From force many endeavours have been used, either to dissuade, or to deter us. Sometimes the merit of the Americans is exalted, and sometimes their sufferings are aggravated. We are told of their contributions to the last war, a war incited by their outcries, and continued for their protection, a war by which none but themselves were gainers. All that they can boast is, that they did some-

Taxation No Tyranny

thing for themselves, and did not wholly stand inactive, while the sons of Britain were fighting in their cause.

If we cannot admire, we are called to pity them; to pity those that shew no regard to their mother-country; have obeyed no law which they could violate; have imparted no good which they could withhold; have entered into associations of fraud to rob their creditors; and into combinations to distress all who depended on their commerce. We are reproached with the cruelty of shutting one port, where every port is shut against us. We are censured as tyrannical for hindering those from fishing, who have condemned our merchants to bankruptcy and our manufacturers to hunger.

Others persuade us to give them more liberty, to take off restraints, and relax authority; and tell us what happy consequences will arise from forbearance: How their affections will be conciliated, and into what diffusions of beneficence their gratitude will luxuriate. They will love their friends. They will reverence their protectors. They will throw themselves into our arms, and lay their property at our feet. They will buy from no other what we can sell them; they will sell to no other what we wish to buy.

That any obligations should overpower their attention to profit, we have known them long enough not to expect. It is not to be expected from a more liberal people. With what kindness they repay benefits, they are now shewing us, who, as soon as we have delivered them from France, are defying and proscribing us.

But if we will permit them to tax themselves, they will give us more than we require. If we proclaim them independent, they will during pleasure pay us a subsidy. The contest is not now for money, but for power. The question is not how much we shall collect, but by what authority the collection shall be made.

Those who find that the Americans cannot be shewn in any form that may raise love or pity, dress them in habiliments of terrour, and try to make us think them formidable. The Bostonians can call into the field ninety thousand men. While we conquer all before us, new enemies will rise up behind, and our work will be always to begin. If we take possession of the towns, the Colonists will retire into the inland regions, and the gain of victory will be only empty houses and a wide extent of waste and desolation. If we subdue them for the present, they will universally revolt in the next war, and resign us without pity to subjection and destruction.

Taxation No Tyranny

To all this it may be answered, that between losing America and resigning it, there is no great difference; that it is not very reasonable to jump into the sea, because the ship is leaky. All those evils may befal us, but we need not hasten them.

The Dean of Gloucester has proposed, and seems to propose it seriously, that we should at once release our claims, declare them masters of themselves, and whistle them down the wind. His opinion is, that our gain from them will be the same, and our expence less. What they can have most cheaply from Britain, they will still buy, what they can sell to us at the highest price they will still sell.

It is, however, a little hard, that having so lately fought and conquered for their safety, we should govern them no longer. By letting them loose before the war, how many millions might have been saved. One wild proposal is best answered by another. Let us restore to the French what we have taken from them. We shall see our Colonists at our feet, when they have an enemy so near them. Let us give the Indians arms, and teach them discipline, and encourage them now and then to plunder a Plantation. Security and leisure are the parents of sedition.

While these different opinions are agitated, it seems to be determined by the Legislature, that force shall be tried. Men of the pen have seldom any great skill in conquering kingdoms, but they have strong inclination to give advice. I cannot forbear to wish, that this commotion may end without bloodshed, and that the rebels may be subdued by terrour rather than by violence; and therefore recommend such a force as may take away, not only the power, but the hope of resistance, and by conquering without a battle, save many from the sword.

If their obstinacy continues without actual hostilities, it may perhaps be mollified by turning out the soldiers to free quarters, forbidding any personal cruelty or hurt. It has been proposed, that the slaves should be set free, an act which surely the lovers of liberty cannot but recommend. If they are furnished with fire-arms for defence, and utensils for husbandry, and settled in some simple form of government within the country, they may be more grateful and honest than their masters.

Far be it from any Englishman to thirst for the blood of his fellow-subjects. Those who most deserve our resentment are unhappily at less distance. The Americans, when the Stamp Act was first proposed, undoubtedly disliked it, as every nation dislikes an impost; but they had no thought of resisting it, till they were encouraged and incited by European intelligence from men whom they thought their friends, but who were friends only to themselves.

On the original contrivers of mischief let an insulted nation pour out its vengeance. With whatever design they have inflamed this pernicious contest, they are themselves equally detestable: If they wish success to the Colonies, they are traitors to this country, if they wish their defeat, they are traitors at once to America and England. To them and them only must be imputed the interruption of commerce, and the miseries of war, the sorrow of those that shall be ruined, and the blood of those that shall fall.

Since the Americans have made it necessary to subdue them, may they be subdued with the least injury possible to their persons and their possessions. When they are reduced to obedience, may that obedience be secured by stricter laws and stronger obligations.

Nothing can be more noxious to society, than that erroneous clemency, which, when a rebellion is suppressed, exacts no forfeiture and establishes no securities, but leaves the rebels in their former state. Who would not try the experiment which promises advantage without expence? If rebels once obtain a victory, their wishes are accomplished; if they are defeated, they suffer little, perhaps less than their conquerors; however often they play the game, the chance is always in their favour. In the mean time, they are growing rich by victualing the troops that we have sent against them, and perhaps gain more by the residence of the army than they lose by the obstruction of their port.

Their charters being now, I suppose, legally forfeited, may be modelled as shall appear most commodious to the Mother-country. Thus the privileges, which are found by experience liable to misuse, will be taken away, and those who now bellow as patriots, bluster as soldiers, and domineer as legislators, will sink into sober merchants and silent planters, peaceably diligent, and securely rich.

But there is one writer, and perhaps many who do not write, to whom the contraction of these pernicious privileges appears very dangerous, and who startle at the thoughts of *England free and America in chains*. Children fly from their own shadow, and rhetori-

Taxation No Tyranny

cians are frighted by their own voices. *Chains* is undoubtedly a dreadful word; but perhaps the masters of civil wisdom may discover some gradations between chains and anarchy. Chains need not be put upon those who will be restrained without them. This contest may end in the softer phrase of English Superiority and American Obedience.

We are told, that the subjection of Americans may tend to the diminution of our own liberties: an event, which none but very perspicacious politicians are able to foresee. If slavery be thus fatally contagious, how is it that we hear the loudest yelps for liberty among the drivers of negroes?

But let us interrupt a while this dream of conquest, settlement, and supremacy. Let us remember that being to contend, according to one orator, with three millions of Whigs, and according to another, with ninety thousand patriots of Massachuset's Bay, we may possibly be checked in our career of reduction. We may be reduced to peace upon equal terms, or driven from the western continent, and forbidden to violate a second time the happy borders of the land of liberty. The time is now perhaps at hand, which Sir Thomas Brown predicted between jest and earnest,

> *When America shall no more send out her treasure,*
> *But spend it at home in American pleasure.*

If we are allowed upon our defeat to stipulate conditions, I hope the treaty of Boston will permit us to import into the confederated Cantons such products as they do not raise, and such manufactures as they do not make, and cannot buy cheaper from other nations, paying like others the appointed customs; that if an English ship salutes a fort with four guns, it shall be answered at least with two; and that if an Englishman be inclined to hold a plantation, he shall only take an oath of allegiance to the reigning powers, and be suffered, while he lives inoffensively, to retain his own opinion of English rights, unmolested in his conscience by an oath of abjuration.

Notes

The following abbreviations have been used:

Congress *Journals of the Continental Congress, 1774–1789*, ed. W. C. Ford, *et al.*, 1904–37, vol. I. [For contemporary editions of *Extracts from the Votes and Proceedings v.* ibid., pp. 131 f.]
DNB *Dictionary of National Biography.*
EHD *English Historical Documents*, gen. ed. D. C. Douglas, 1953– .
GM *The Gentleman's Magazine.*
Life *Boswell's Life of Johnson*, ed. G. B. Hill, rev. L. F. Powell, 1934–50.
OED *Oxford English Dictionary.*
Parl. Hist. *The Parliamentary History of England*, ed. W. Cobbett, 1806–20.
P.R.O. Public Record Office.

I AN INTRODUCTION TO THE POLITICAL STATE OF GREAT-BRITAIN

page	line	
1	1	'pamphlet': i.e. *Literary Magazine,* in which *Introduction to the Political State of Great-Britain* was first article.
	11 f.	Acts of Supremacy and Uniformity 1559; adoption of Thirty-Nine Articles 1563.
	19	Voyages during Elizabeth's reign preceded successful colonisation of next.
	21–2	Aztec capital captured by Cortés 1521, Inca capital by Pizarro 1533. Rich vein of silver at Potosi discovered 1545.
2	10–12	Pope Alexander VI's Bull (1493) assigned to Spain and Portugal right of discovery and possession westward and eastward from imaginary line across Atlantic.
	13	Philip II of Spain ruled Portugal 1580–98.
	21–3	Revolt of Netherlands 1568–1648. Leicester sent to help Dutch 1585–7.
	34–5	Dutch East India Company founded 1602, Dutch West India Company 1621.

Notes

page	line	
3	8 f.	Having claimed throne 1589, Henry of Navarre crowned 1594. Religious Wars 1562–93; Edict of Nantes 1598 gave Huguenots some rights. Credited with intention of building up series of alliances to destroy rival House of Hapsburg, Henry assassinated 1610 by fanatic Ravaillac.
4	4	Mary Stuart, daughter of James V of Scotland and Mary of Guise, married dauphin Francis 1558.
	25–7	James I failed to give Protestant son-in-law Frederick V, Elector Palatine, active support against Ferdinand II and Catholic League.
5	8–9	Settlements at Jamestown 1607, Plymouth 1620.
	16–17	Buckingham sent to island of Rhé 1627, but fleet failed to relieve La Rochelle, centre of Huguenot disaffection, which capitulated 1628.
	22	First levy of ship-money in peacetime 1634; further levies, extended to inland towns, 1635, 1636, 1639. English Civil War 1642–6.
6	4–5	Champlain founded Quebec 1608; appointed Governor of New France 1632. Colony placed under French Crown 1663.
7	6–7	Cromwell defeated Royalists at Naseby 1645; Colonel Pride 'purged' House of Commons 1648.
	9	First Anglo-Dutch War 1652–4.
	19 f.	War between England and Spain 1656–9. Penn and Venables captured Jamaica 1655.
8	12–13	Treaty of Paris 1657 between England and France against Spain, who by Treaty of Pyrenees 1659 obliged to cede frontier fortresses in Flanders to France.
	25–6	Conflict between army and parliament after Cromwell's death (Sept. 1658) led to re-establishment of Long Parliament (Feb. 1660) and proclamation of Charles as King in May (*v. EHD*, VIII. 58–9).
	32	Carolinas settled 1665, 1670, Pennsylvania 1681.
	38–9	Second Anglo-Dutch War 1665–7.
9	1–2	War between France and Netherlands 1672–8.
	25	Colbert, Comptroller-General of France 1661–83.
	38	Louis XIV (1643–1715).
11	5	Large immigration into New France during Louis XIV's reign. *Compagnie des Indes Orientales* founded 1664.
	14	Wars of Devolution 1667–8, against Netherlands 1672–8, of League of Augsburg 1688–97, of Spanish Succession 1701–14.

Notes

page	line	
11	20	Rebellion of Monmouth and Argyle 1685 after James II ascended throne.
	31–2	Under William and Mary England joined other Protestant powers in League of Augsburg against France.
12	4	English fleet defeated at Beachy Head 1690.
	5–6	By English and Dutch 1692.
	30–1	William defeated at Steinkirk 1692, Neerwinden 1693.
	36	Treaty of Ryswyck 1697 (*v. EHD*, VIII. 881–3).
13	5	England entered War of Spanish Succession 1702. Gibraltar captured 1704, Barcelona 1705, Minorca 1708.
	14–15	French defeated at Blenheim 1704, Ramillies 1706, Oudenarde 1708, Malplaquet 1709.
	21 f.	Attack on Quebec defeated 1711 with loss of ten ships.
	24	Sailing Sept. 1740 to attack Spanish Pacific settlements, Anson's squadron severely buffeted by storms off Cape Horn.
	28–9	Whigs opposed Peace of Utrecht 1713 (for articles of which *v. EHD*, VIII. 885–9).
	32	England's alliance with France 1717 reaffirmed by Treaty of Hanover 1725.
14	6	Navigation Acts excluded foreign shipping and manufactures from British colonial trade (cf. *EHD*, IX. 353 f., 414–15).
	15 f.	La Salle took possession of Mississippi valley in name of French King 1682; Louisiana founded 1699.
	25–6	Newfoundland discovered 1497.
	32	Georgia founded 1732.
15	36	Forts Rouillé 1749, Le Boeuf 1753, Duquesne 1754.
16	12–13	French and Indian War 1755–63. Braddock routed by Indians and French during march on Fort Duquesne 1755.

2 OBSERVATIONS ON HIS BRITANNIC MAJESTY'S TREATIES

18	1	Treaties with Hesse-Cassel and Russia signed at Hanover and St. Petersburg respectively on 18 June and 30 Sept. 1755.
19	20–2	Cf. Samuel Martin, *Deliberate Thoughts on the System of our late Treaties with Hesse-Cassell and Russia in regard to Hanover* (1756), p. 14.
20	3 f.	*v. Treaty between his Britannick Majesty and Her Imperial Majesty of All the Russias* (signed Moscow 11 Dec. 1742

Notes

page	line	
		and confirmed by later treaty), art. XV (*Literary Magazine*, I. 115); also Hesse-Cassel treaty, art. IX (ibid., I. 117).
20	22	i.e. Hanover. Cf. Martin, p. 13.
	31	Act of Settlement 1701 (*v. EHD*, VIII. 129–35).
22	1	Militia Bill introduced Mar. 1756.

3 OBSERVATIONS ON THE PRESENT STATE OF AFFAIRS

23	21–2	French and Indian War began with dispute over Ohio valley.
26	37	War of Austrian Succession 1740–8 concluded by Treaty of Aix-la-Chapelle.
27	10	*v.* note to p. 15, l. 36.
28	9	Nova Scotia (formerly French Arcadia) conquered by British 1710, colonised as defensive bastion 1749.
	37 f.	English planters dispossessed by French from Martinique 1723.
29	12–13	War between England and Spain (War of Jenkins' Ear) 1739–48.
	17	Pragmatic Army defeated French at Dettingen 1743.
	18	Fontenoy 1745. D. J. Greene kindly informs me that Val is better known in history as Lauffeld, an engagement of 1747; cf. *The Politics of Samuel Johnson*, pp. 36, 296, n. 27.
	19–20	Admiral Matthews' failure to pursue French and Spanish fleets off Toulon 1744 was regarded as national disgrace. Two French convoys were successfully attacked in 1747.
	26	Louisburg capitulated June 1745.
	29–30	i.e. during the Forty-five Rebellion.
	35	Fort St. George (Madras) surrendered to French Sept. 1746.
30	27	Louis XV (1715–74).

4 OBSERVATIONS (AUGUST–SEPTEMBER 1758)

32	21	Attacks on Rochefort 1757, St. Malo and Cherbourg 1758, and Belleisle 1761, weakened French war-effort against Frederick II of Prussia and Ferdinand of Brunswick.
33	19	Capture of Minorca 1756 released French Mediterranean fleet for service elsewhere.

Notes

page	line	
33	25–6	In *Idler* 20 (26 Aug. 1758) Johnson deplores lack of truthful impartiality among historians, imagining how differently the capture of Louisburg will be represented by future English and French historians.
	27 f.	Fortress fell to English and colonial forces after two-month siege.
34	21	In Moravia Frederick raised siege of Olmutz (July) after enemy cut his supply-lines.
35	12–13	News of Frederick's victory over invading Russian army at Zorndorf (25 Aug.) had not reached England at time of writing.
	29 f.	Royal procession of French colours captured at Louisburg from Kensington Palace to St. Paul's included 80 each of Horse and Life Guards.
36	7	*Ovation*: 'a lesser triumph among the Romans allowed to those who had won a victory without much bloodshed, or defeated some less formidable enemy' (Johnson's *Dictionary*).
	11 f.	v. note to p. 13, ll. 14–15.
37	10	Throughout Johnson quotes from letter (dated 9, published 16 Sept.) attacking his previous 'observation'.
38	6	French fortress on L. Champlain.
	32	Dunkirk surrendered to English 1658; resold to France 1662. Treaty of Utrecht stipulated demolition of fortifications and occupation by English garrison.

5 THE FALSE ALARM

40	7–8	Cf. George Rudé, *Wilkes and Liberty: A Social Study of 1763 to 1774* (1962), p. 105: 'The 60,000 petitioners must ... have accounted for something more than a quarter of the total voting population.'
	16 f.	Commons voted (15 Apr. 1769) Henry Lawes Luttrell elected for Middlesex, though John Wilkes (previously declared 'incapable of being elected a member to serve in this present parliament') had defeated him at poll.
	23–4	Martial, VI. xix. 1–2 ('My action is not one for assault, or bloodshed, or poisoning: it concerns three she-goats').
	28–9	Wilkes imprisoned June 1768 till Apr. 1770 for earlier *North Briton* 45 and *Essay on Woman*, and expelled second time from Commons 3 Feb. 1769 for these and

Notes

page	line	
		so-called libellous preface implying Weymouth's letter responsible for the 'Massacre' of St. George's Fields.
40	37–8	Returns for City of London (Mar. 1768) placed Wilkes bottom of poll.
41	12 f.	Cf. Sir William Meredith, *The Question Stated* (1769), pp. 11–12, 17–18.
	32	In 1642 Commons refused to arrest Pym, Hampden, Holles, Hazelrigg, Strode.
	38–9	By Junius in *Public Advertiser*, 19 Dec. 1769; v. *The Letters of Junius*, ed. C. W. Everett (1927), pp. 141, 146–7.
42	14	i.e. Arthur Hall (v. *DNB*).
	27–8	v. Sir William Blackstone, *Commentaries on the Laws of England* (1765–9), I. 169; cf. Meredith, pp. 22–4.
43	11	Wilkes previously expelled from Parliament 20 Jan. 1764.
	12–13	*Parl. Hist.*, XVI. 545; *EHD*, X. 170.
	16–18	On 2 Feb. 1769 and 18 June 1768 respectively.
	24 f.	*Parl. Hist.*, XVI. 577; *EHD*, X. 171.
	37–8	On 17 Mar.
45	21–2	Cf. Selden's account of case of Richard Lions. *The Priviledges of the Baronage of England* (1642), pp. 34–40.
	28	For argument Johnson here answering cf. Meredith, p. 20.
46	17 f.	Cf. Downley and Dunning, *The Sentiments of an English Freeholder on the late Decision of the Middlesex Election* (1769), p. 2; George Grenville, *The Speech of a Right Honourable Gentleman on the Motion for expelling Mr. Wilkes* (1769), p. 32.
	26	This point had been widely disputed; v. *A Fair Trial of the Important Question* (1769); also Grenville, p. 32; Meredith, p. 55; *Letters of Junius*, pp. 74 f.
47	4	Cf. Downley and Dunning, pp. 24–5; also Grenville, p. 30, Meredith, p. 58.
49	16–17	'Quem deus vult perdere prius dementat.'
	19–20	For phrase 'alarming crisis' cf. *Letters of Junius*, p. 53; *Parl. Hist.*, XVI. 748 (Chatham).
	27 f.	Meredith, p. 46: '... if a Vote of the House is self-sufficient for the Purpose, those Acts are all frivolous; nor would the House of Commons have endured their being brought in at all; for they are too jealous of their Privileges to suffer the other Parts of the Legislature to interfere, where they claim an *exclusive* Jurisdiction'.

Notes

page	line	
49	36 f.	First Test Act 1673 (*v. EHD*, VIII. 389–91); South Sea Bubble 1720.
50	9–10	Special exception then made in favour of Sir Francis Bacon.
	24 f.	i.e. during debate on William Dowdeswell's amendment (defeated) to have words of vote expelling Wilkes added to motion of 7 Feb. (*Parl. Hist.*, XVI. 579).
	30–1	Cf. *Sir Henry Cavendish's Debates of the House of Commons 1768–1774*, ed. J. Wright (1840), p. 233 (17 Feb. 1769).
	36 f.	Cf. Meredith, pp. 59–62; also Downley and Dunning, p. 55.
51	9	Pro-Wilkite Society of Supporters of Bill of Rights founded 20 Feb. 1769. (Bill of Rights, 1689.)
53	28–9	*Chevy Chase*, ll. 239–40, quoted in Parliament by Lord Strange 17 Feb. 1769 (*Cavendish's Debates*, p. 228). With sentiments of Johnson's paragraph cf. *An Address to the People of England on the Inexpediency of Dissolving the Present Parliament* (1770).
55	24	Yorkshire petition contained nearly 11,000 signatures. Probably no Cumberland petition presented, though one feared as late as Jan. 1770.
56	5–6	Window-tax, originally imposed 1696, increased by numerous later acts (cf. *EHD*, VIII. 309–11; X. 317–19).
	7	Several petitions demanded dissolution of Parliament.
	37–8	*v.* John Norris, *Shelburne and Reform* (1963), p. 72; Rudé, pp. 129–31, 138 f.
57	5 f.	*Paradise Lost*, VI. 621–7.
	15	Peasants' Revolt 1381.
	22–3	*Jacquerie* 1358.
	32–4	Edward McQuirk acquitted by royal pardon (Mar. 1769) of murder of George Clark at Brentford election (Dec. 1768) following inquiry by Surgeons' Company. For public 'clamour' cf. *St. James's Chronicle*, 7, 9, 18 Mar. (*Letters of Junius*, pp. 46–9); also William Moore, *A Paper on the late extraordinary Proceedings, and the Miraculous Device, and Determination of the Butchers Company* (22 Mar. 1769).
	36–7	Cf. *Letters of Junius*, pp. 135–48.
58	4	Non-jurors refused to take oaths of allegiance and supremacy 1689.
	7–8	*v. The Kings Cabinet Opened*, published by special order of the Parliament (1645), sigs. A3–4ᵛ.

Notes

page	line	
58	12	Conspiracy of Catiline 63–2 B.C.
	15	Wat Tyler; Robert Kett executed as rebel 1549 (v. DNB).
	21	i.e. James Francis Edward, the Old Pretender.
	32	Juvenal, Satires, X. 64 ('. . . there are being made pipkins, basins, frying-pans and little dishes').

6 THOUGHTS ON THE LATE TRANSACTIONS RESPECTING FALKLAND'S ISLANDS

60	19	Caesar crossed Rubicon 49 B.C.
61	15	'Hanseatic league': loose aggregation or *firma confederatio* of German towns for trade.
	23	v. p. 14, l. 23, and note.
	26–7	Drake circumnavigated world 1577–80; Magellan named Pacific (1520) on earlier voyage.
	38–9	v. *The Voyages and Works of John Davis*, ed. A. H. Markham for Hakluyt Society (1880), p. 108 and note.
62	5–6	*The Observations of Sir Richard Hawkins* (1662), p. 70.
	14–15	A. F. Frézier, *A Voyage to the South-Sea and along the Coasts of Chili and Peru in 1712, 1713, 1714*, translated from the French (1717), p. 287.
	17	For early copies of Journal of John Strong, Commander of 'Welfare', v. British Museum MSS. Harley 5101; Sloane 3295.
	18	Edmond Halley, *Atlas maritimus & commercialis* (1728), chart 47 (where 'Sebaldo de Wort Is' and 'Falkland Is' shown as distinct).
	22–4	MS. Harley 5101, f. 14^v; William Dampier, *A New Voyage round the World* (1697), p. 81.
	25 f.	Frézier, p. 289.
	33 f.	*A Voyage round the World by George Anson*, compiled Richard Walter, rev. Benjamin Robins (1748), pp. 90–1.
63	8–9	v. note to p. 13, l. 24.
	28 f.	Sir John Narborough et al., *An Account of Several late Voyages & Discoveries to the South and North* (1694), p. 110.
64	27	Richard Wall (1694–1778) statesman in Spanish service (v. DNB).
	36	José de Carvajal y Lancáster (1698–1754).
65	23	Egmont appointed First Lord of Admiralty Sept. 1763.
	32 f.	John Byron's Journal of 'Dolphin' (1764–6) in National

Notes

page	line	
		Maritime Museum (MS. 57/053) mentions '60 or 70 fine Geese' (f. 79). Johnson's details also differ slightly from published accounts: *v. A Voyage round the World by Commodore Byron*, by an Officer on Board (1767), pp. 70–6; *An Account of the Voyages for making Discoveries in the Southern Hemisphere*, ed. John Hawkesworth (1773), pp. 47–54. Byron's letter (24 Feb. 1765) to Egmont in P.R.O. S.P. Spain Supplementary, 253.
66	12 f.	*v.* John McBride to Egmont, 6 Apr. 1766, P.R.O. Adm. 1. 2116.
	20	South American Indians represented by travellers as of gigantic proportions; cf. Johnson's *Journey to the Western Islands of Scotland* (1775), p. 277.
67	4	Horace, *Odes*, I. iii. 37.
	19 f.	For correspondence providing account of these events *v. Papers relative to the Taking of Port Egmont and Falkland's Island from the English, State Papers* (1777), pt. II, pp. 10–11, 13, 15–22, 27–34. (Originals in P.R.O.)
69	9	400 bombs listed among Spanish armament (ibid., p. 35).
	39 f.	Cf. ibid., pp. 36 f. (Articles of Capitulation); pp. 40–1 (Inventory).
70	24 f.	For correspondence providing account of these transactions *v. Papers relative to the late Negotiation with Spain, State Papers* (1777), pt. I, pp. 5–7, 10–11, 14, 17–18, 21–2, 27–32. (Originals in P.R.O.) Rochford succeeded Weymouth as Secretary of State for Southern Department 18 Dec. 1770.
73	12–13	Choiseul dismissed as Minister of War 24 Dec. 1770.
	37 f.	*v.* op. cit., p. 32; *GM*, XLI (1771), 2.
74	29	*Greek Calends*: 'never'; cf. Thomas Blount, *Glossographia* (1656): 'At the Greek Calends, never; for the Greeks have no Calends.'
	30–2	*De facto* independence dating from Peace of Basle (1499) not formally recognised till 1648.
75	3	i.e. Chatham; *v. Parl. Hist.*, XVI. 1094–5, 1339, 1355, 1380–5.
	10 f.	*Vers sur le Cardinal de Richelieu*, of which Johnson misquotes first two lines:

> 'Qu' on parle mal ou bien du fameux Cardinal,
> Ma prose ni mes vers n' en diront jamais rien . . .'

| 76 | 2–3 | *Letters of Junius*, p. 186. |

Notes

page	line	
76	24 f.	This sentence added 1776. British expedition withdrew 1774.
	36–7	*Historia Placitorum Coronae: The History of the Pleas of the Crown* (1736), pp. 25–7.
	38	Ovid, *Metamorphoses*, I. 190.
77	15–16	Addison, *The Campaign*, ll. 313–14, misquoted.
78	35–6	After dismissal of Choiseul, Chancellor Maupeou pursued policy of destroying power of *parlements*.
79	27	France ceded Canada to England by Treaty of Paris (*v. EHD*, X. 937–8).
	28	i.e. Chatham; *v. Parl. Hist.*, XV. 1266–7; cf. O. A. Sherrard, *Lord Chatham and America* (1958), p. 31.
80	2–3	*v.* p. 61; Hawkyns died 1595 and Drake 1596 during an unprofitable expedition against Spanish West Indies and Central America.
	10–12	*v.* note to p. 7, ll. 19 f.
	14	i.e. in 1741.
	20–2	Disease took heavy toll of British during forty-five-day siege of Havana (1762). Johnson lost his friend Dr. Richard Bathurst in expedition; *v. Life*, I. 242, n. 1, 382.
81	11–12	*v. Letters of Junius*, p. 186.
	38	Ibid., p. 190.
82	1	Vergil, *Aeneid*, II. 97–9.
	2–3	*Julius Caesar*, III. i. 274.
	9	*v.* E. Cobham Brewer, *A Dictionary of Phrase and Fable* (1923), p. 603; *English Fairy Tales*, ed. E. S. Hartland (1893), pp. 3 f.
	18	Identity still debated; *v.* Alvar Ellegård, *Who Was Junius?* (1962); *A Statistical Method for Determining Authorship: The 'Junius' Letters, 1769–1772* (1962); J. N. M. MacLean, *Reward is Secondary: The Life of a Political Adventurer and an Inquiry into the Mystery of 'Junius'* (1963); also reviews and correspondence in *Times Literary Supplement* (1963), p. 67, 1009, 1054.
83	2–3	George Bellas (*d.* 1776) pro-Wilkite alderman; William Beckford (1709–70) presented as Lord Mayor an arrogantly worded remonstrance to the King on Middlesex election.
	20	*Dunciad*, III. 208.
	22	Brass Crosby (1725–93), John Sawbridge (1732–95), James Townsend (1737–87), members of Bill of Rights Society who espoused Wilkes' cause in Commons.

Notes

page	line	
84	11	Manila ransomed after capture 1762, but bills on Spanish treasury rejected at Madrid. Cf. *Letters of Junius*, p. 33, n. 2.
86	6–8	Cf. ibid., pp. 187, 189–90.
87	14 f.	Grenville became First Lord of Treasury Apr. 1763, Rockingham July 1765.
	18–20	1st issue of 1st edn. contained famous sarcasm on Grenville: 'Let him not, however, be depreciated in his grave; he had powers not universally possessed; if he could have got the money, he could have counted it.'
88	31–2	*Paradise Lost*, IX. 463–6.
	35	Cf. *Letters of Junius*, p. 186.
89	8	Bill of Rights Society was influential in Surrey, Rockingham Whigs in Derbyshire and Yorkshire. All three counties presented petitions on Wilkes' behalf.
	25–6	'A morbid condition of the body in which lice multiply excessively, causing extreme irritation' (*OED*).

7 THE PATRIOT

91	7–8	Parliament dissolved 30 Sept. 1774 before its full term.
92	8	Cf. Hobbes, *Leviathan*, I. xvi; James Burgh, *Political Disquisitions* (1774–5), I. 3.
	32–4	Wilkes elected Lord Mayor and took his seat as M.P. for Middlesex 1774.
93	16 f.	Opposition hinted at improper relationship between Bute and King's mother. v. also *Middlesex Journal*, 15 Oct. 1774 (letter from 'A Friend to the Public'); Burgh, I. 196–7; *Letters of Junius*, pp. 173, 178, 180; Rudé, p. 186.
	24	Cf. *Parl. Hist.*, XVII. 1403 (Chatham). For Quebec Act v. *EHD*, X. 787–91; Sir Reginald Coupland, *The Quebec Act* (1925); Bernard Donoughue, *British Politics and the American Revolution* (1964), pp. 105–26.
	38–9	v. note to p. 79, l. 27; *GM*, XXXIII (1763), 122 (art. IV).
94	2	Religious liberty proposed for Irish Catholics by Treaty of Limerick 1691 (v. *EHD*, VIII. 765).
	3	Cf. *Life*, II. 249; IV. 216.
	17–18	'Such as a man's company, such his manners' (1622).
	28	*burning a boot*: 'A jackboot and a petticoat, the popular

page	line	
		emblems of Bute [pronounced as "boot"] and the princess, were frequently burnt by excited mobs' (*DNB*).
94	29	On 26 Sept. 1774 Wilkes addressed large meeting of freeholders at Mile End, pledging himself to shorter parliaments and electoral reform; *v*. Donoughue, p. 196. *Lumber-Troop*: 'A convivial society of London citizens (dissolved in 1859), with a quasi-military organization, its president being styled the "colonel" ' (*OED*). Cf. title-page of E. Ward's *A Compleat and Humorous Account of all the Remarkable Clubs and Societies in the Cities of London and Westminster, from the R——l S——y down to the Lumber-Troop &c.* (1745 edn.).
95	4–6	Cf. *Middlesex Journal*, 4 Oct. 1774 ('Postscript'): *London Packet*, 10 Oct. 1774 (leader from 'A Liveryman'); Norris, p. 65.
	36 f.	*v. Thoughts on the Late Transactions respecting Falkland's Islands.*
96	16 f.	*v. Taxation No Tyranny.*
	37 f.	Cf. *Parl. Hist.*, XVII. 1354. For Boston Port Act *v. EHD*, IX, 780–1.
97	30–2	Ban on publication of parliamentary debates relaxed 1771; Grenville's Controverted Elections Act 1770 (*v. EHD*, X. 188–91).
99	8–9	*Paradise Lost*, II. 5–6.

8 TAXATION NO TYRANNY

101	22 f.	Both views expressed by Chatham, *Parl. Hist.*, XVIII. 149 f.
102	1 f.	*v. Parl. Hist.*, XVII. 1236 (Burke); 1355 (Chatham).
	11 f.	Cf. ibid., XVI. 104; XVII. 1353; XVIII. 154. 'In the debates on the Coercion Acts [of 1774] most people, Opposition as well as Administration, usually ignored the specific measures and discussed the Parliamentary *right* to tax' (Donoughue, p. 53, n. 1).
	19–20	*The Letters of Governor Hutchinson and Lieut. Governor Oliver . . . and Remarks thereon, with the Assembly's Address and the Proceedings of the Lords Committee of Council* (1774), p. 123; cf. Greene, p. 321, n. 79.
	31	*Hydra*: 'The fabulous many-headed snake of the marshes of Lerna, whose heads grew again as fast as they were cut

Notes

page	line	
		off: said to have been at length killed by Hercules' (*OED*). The Hydra was destroyed by fire and the sword, Hercules cutting off the heads while his charioteer Iolaus seared the stumps with burning brands.
102	36–7	*v.* John Dickinson, *The Late Regulations respecting the British Colonies . . . Considered* (1765); *Parl. Hist.*, XVI. 105–6; Matthew Robinson-Morris, *Considerations on the Measures carrying on with respect to the British Colonies in North-America* (1774). Cf. *EHD*, IX. 392 f.
103	16 f.	*v. Parl. Hist.*, XVIII. 195–8.
	25 f.	Chatham (quoting opinion of Benjamin Franklin), ibid., XVIII. 153.
	37–9	*Extracts from the Votes and Proceedings* (London, 1774), p. 9.
104	16	Addison, *Letter from Italy*, l. 120.
	25–7	Cf. *Parl. Hist.*, XVI. 99–100; G. H. Guttridge, *English Whiggism and the American Revolution* (reprinted 1963), pp. 65–6.
105	29	Cf. conversation between Descartes and third False Demetrius in *Dialogues des Morts*.
106	1 f.	A counter-argument to Thomas Jefferson's *A Summary View of the Rights of British America* (1774), pp. 7–8.
108	3	Sea-route to India discovered by Vasco da Gama 1497–9, America by Columbus 1492, though mainland of South America sighted for first time 1498.
	13	*v.* Thomas Fuller, *The History of the Worthies of England* (1662), p. 258; cf. George Peele, *The Battle of Alcazar* (1594), where Stukley describes himself as born in London (sig. F3ᵛ).
110	38 f.	*v. Parl. Hist.*, XVI. 161 f.; *EHD*, IX. 644, 696; cf. John Dickinson, *Letters from a Farmer in Pensylvania to the Inhabitants of the British Colonies* (1768), pp. 17–18; *Congress*, pp. 91–2.
111	6–8	Cf. *Parl. Hist.*, XVI. 99–100; Arthur Lee, *An Appeal to the Justice and Interests of the People of Great Britain, by an Old Member of Parliament* (1776, 4th edn.), pp. 20–2.
	30–1	*Congress*, p. 110; *The Spirit of Laws*, IX. 6.
112	35 f.	In this section of pamphlet Johnson quotes from first four and 7th resolutions of Continental Congress held at Philadelphia; *v. Congress*, pp. 67, 68–9.
114	16	Virgil, *Eclogues*, X. 5. ('Briny Doris may not mingle her wave with thine.')

Notes

page	line	
114	38	Note added by Johnson in 1776: 'Of this reasoning, I owe part to a conversation with Sir John Hawkins.'
115	20	Thomas Cushing (1725–88), speaker of the Massachusetts House of Representatives, member of the Committee of Safety, Massachusetts' representative at Continental Congress.
116	7 f.	v. *The Charters of the . . . Provinces of North America* (1766), 'Pensylvania Charter', p. 5 (v. *EHD*, IX. 100).
	24–6	Josiah Tucker (Dean of Gloucester), *Four Tracts together with Two Sermons on Political and Commercial Subjects* (1774), 97 note.
	27 f.	*The Political and Commercial Works of . . . Charles D'Avenant, LL.D.*, ed. C. Whitworth (1774), II. 240.
	32	Cf. note to p. 102, ll. 11 f.; *Parl. Hist.*, XVI. 178 (Camden: 'Taxation and representation are inseparable'); XVIII. 204 (Chatham); Lee, p. 10.
117	12	For this and subsequent references to the 'Old Member' v. Lee, pp. 24, 32–3, 12–15, 17.
118	7	v. *The Statutes at Large*, ed. Owen Ruffhead, rev. Charles Runnington (1786–1800), V. 179; *EHD*, X. 683.
	9 f.	*Parl. Hist.*, XVI. 104 (Pitt in answer to Grenville); Lee, p. 19.
119	5 f.	v. *Parl. Hist.*, XVI. 100; XVII. 1355–6; XVIII. 154; Francis Maseres, *Considerations on the Expediency of Admitting Representatives from the American Colonies into the British House of Commons* (1770).
120	2–3	'Circular Letter from Selectmen of Boston' (14 Sept. 1768), *Report of the Lords Committees appointed by the House of Lords* (1774), p. 15.
	18–20	*Congress*, pp. 43, 51–2, 76–7. Cf. Donoughue, p. 173. Johnson, in writing 'November' for 'September', probably thinking of date of landing in England.
	21 f.	*Congress*, pp. 77–8, 79, 101.
	38	For references in this and subsequent paragraph v. ibid., pp. 110–112, 83, 112, 82.
121	24–6	Israel Mauduit, *A Short View of the History of the New England Colonies with respect to their Charters and Constitution* (1774, 2nd edn.), pp. 70–1.
	27 f.	For British coercive measures of 1774 v. Introduction, p. xviii; *Congress*, pp. 76, 85–8, 117.
122	6	Cf. *Ars Poetica*, 11, 180–2.
	17 f.	Cf. *Congress*, p. 87.

Notes

page	line	
122	29–31	*Congress*, pp. 84–5.
	39	Ibid., pp. 79–80, 85, 91–2, 93, 96–7, 116.
123	22 f.	Ibid., pp. 88–9.
124	15	*Pactolus:* Lydian river with sands of gold.
125	11–13	Herodotus, IV, 1–4.
126	9	Johnson parodying words of address 'To the People of Great-Britain'; *v. Congress*, p. 82.
	27	Earlier editions had read: 'Independence is the gift of Nature, bestowed impartially on all her sons. No man . . .'.
127	12	Earlier editions had read: 'Our number of legislators was originally a burthen imposed upon us by English tyranny and ought . . .'.
	22	Cf. note to p. 120, ll. 18–20.
128	8–10	*v.* p. 123, ll. 22 f. and note; cf. also *Congress*, p. 82.
	12–13	Addison, *Praelium inter Pygmaeos et Grues Commissum*, ll. 53 f. (Johnson translated this poem into heroic couplets.)
	14–15	*Parl. Hist.*, XVI. 104 (Chatham: 'three millions of people, so dead to all the feelings of liberty, as voluntarily to submit to be slaves, would have been fit instruments to make slaves of the rest').
	20	Thomas Baker, *Reflections upon Learning* (1699), pp. 11–12.
	26–7	Catharine Macaulay, *An Address to the People . . . on the Present Important Crisis of Affairs* (1775), passim.
	36–7	*Congress*, p. 84.
129	9–10	Two Bills blockading American trade and fishery introduced early in 1775; *v.* Donoughue, pp. 221 f.; *Parl. Hist.*, XVIII. 298 f., 411 f.
	12 f.	Cf. *Parl. Hist.*, XVII. 1355–6.
	32–3	Ibid., XVIII. 239 (Wilkes).
130	5 f.	Tucker, pp. 195 f.
	31–2	Sir William Draper, *The Thoughts of a Traveller upon our American Disputes* (1774), p. 21.
131	38–9	Source untraced. D. J. Greene suggests that this is merely Johnson's paraphrase of the opening passage of Congress's address 'To the People of Great Britain' (*v. Congress*, p. 82). Cf. also *A Letter to the Right Honourable Wills Earl of Hillsborough on the Connection between Great Britain and her American Colonies* (1768), where author answers objection frequently heard that 'the

Notes

page	line	
		Colonists must either be Freemen or Slaves; that no medium can be found between Freedom and Slavery; and, consequently, that if Dependence be enforced in the least degree, the Chains of Slavery are rivetted about their necks' (p. 36).
132	7–8	v. *Parl Hist.*, XVI. 104; XVIII. 156; cf. pp. 123, ll. 22 f., 128, ll. 8–10, and notes.
	13–15	v. notes to pp. 102, ll. 11 f., 129, ll. 32–3.
	21–2	*A Prophecy concerning the Future State of Several Nations*, 'The Prophecy', ll. 11–12; v. *The Works of Sir Thomas Browne*, ed. Geoffrey Keynes (1964), III. 104.

Index

I. *Persons and Places referred to in the Text*

Anne, Queen, 13, 48, 58, 62
Anson, George, Lord, 13, 62–3, 64, 65

Baker, Thomas, 128
Beckford, William, 83
Bellas, George, 83
Birmingham, 103
Blenheim, 36
Boston, 96, 103–4, 121–2, 125, 129, 132
Braddock, Edward, 16
Brazil, 26
Browne, Sir Thomas, 132
Bucarelli, Don Francisco, 71, 72, 73, 76, 84, 85, 86, 87
Buenos Aires, 68, 70, 71, 85, 87
Byron, John, 65–6

Cabot, Sebastian, 14, 61
Cadiz, 70, 72
Caesar, 60
Canada, 6, 8, 13, 15, 31, 93
Cape Breton, *v.* Louisburg
Carolina, 8, 120
Carthagena, 80
Carvajal, José de, 64–5
Catiline, 58
Cavendish, Thomas, 61, 80
Charles I, 5, 58, 121
Charles II, 8–9, 11, 48
Charles III (of Spain), 67, 68, 69, 71, 72, 73–4, 84, 85, 86, 87

Charles Edward, the 'Young Pretender', 29
Chatham, *v.* Pitt
Cherbourg, 32, 38
Chester, 118
Choiseul, Duc de, 73
Colbert, Jean-Baptiste, 9–10
Columbus, Christopher, 14, 61, 107
Corneille, Pierre, 75
Cornwall, 125–8
Cromwell, Oliver, 7–8, 80
Crosby, Brass, 83
Cumberland, 55
Cushing, Thomas, 115

Dampier, William, 62
Davenant, Charles, 116
Davys, John, 61
Derbyshire, 89
Dettingen, 29
Drake, Sir Francis, 80
Dunkirk, 38
Durham, 118

Egmont, John Perceval, Earl of, 65
Elizabeth I, 1, 2, 3, 42, 61, 79–80

Falkland Islands, 60 f., 96
Farmer, George, 68, 69
Fontenelle, Bernard Le Bovier de, 105

Index

Fontenoy, 29
Forts St. George (Madras), 29
  Ticonderoga, 38
Frederick II (of Prussia), 34–5
Frézier, Amédée François, 62

George I, 118
George II, 18, 20
George III, 40, 55, 57–8, 59, 65, 67, 72, 74, 88, 89, 93, 122, 128
Georgia, 14
Gibraltar, 72
Grenville, George, 87
Grimaldi, Marquis de, 71–2, 75, 84

Hale, Sir Matthew, 76
Hall, Arthur, 42
Halley, Edmond, 62
Hanover, 20, 29
Harris, James, 70, 71, 72, 73
Havana, 80
Hawkins, Sir John, 114 n.
Hawkyns, Sir John, 80
Hawkyns, Sir Richard, 62
Henry IV (of France), 3
Henry VII, 14
Hispaniola, 80
Hunt, Anthony, 67–8, 70, 72, 84, 86, 88

Jamaica, 7, 80
James I, 3–4, 121
James II, 11, 58
James Francis Edward, the 'Old Pretender', 58
Junius, 76, 81–3

Keene, Sir Benjamin, 64–5
Kett, Robert, 58

La Hogue, 12

La Rochelle, 5
Lauffeld (Val), 29
Lee, Arthur, 117–18
Limerick, 94
London, 40–1, 82, 89
Louis XIV, 9–10, 11, 93
Louis XV, 30, 73, 78
Louisburg, 29–30, 33–4, 36, 37–8
Louisiana, 14
Luttrell, Henry Lawes, 44, 51

Macaulay, Catherine, 128
McBride, John, 66
McQuirk, Edward, 57
Madariaga, Juan Ignacio, 68–9, 69–70
Madrid, 70, 71, 72, 73
Maltby, William, 68, 70
Manila, 84, 87
Marlborough, John Churchill, Duke of, 13
Maryland, 116
Massachusett's Bay, *v.* Boston
Masserano, Prince, 71, 72, 73–4
Mauduit, Israel, 121
Mexico, 1, 26
Middlesex, 40–1, 43, 47, 51–2, 53, 55, 58, 82, 92
Mile End, 94
Milton, John, 88
Minorca, 33, 36, 37, 38
Molyneux, William, 116
Montesquieu, Charles de Secondat, Baron de, 111

Narborough (or Narbrough), Sir John, 63–4
Naseby, 58
New England, 120
Newfoundland, 14, 15
Nova Scotia, 15, 28

Index

Ohio Valley, 27
Olmutz, 34–5
Oxford, Robert Harley, Earl of, 36

Paris, 27, 32, 33, 36, 37
Penn, Sir William, 7, 26
Pennsylvania, 8, 116, 127, 128
Pepperel, Sir William, 29
Peru, 1, 26
Philadelphia (Congress of), *v.* also Pennsylvania, 115, 120, 123, 125
Philip II (of Spain), 2, 61
Pitt, William, Earl of Chatham, 75, 79, 103, 128, 132
Plymouth, 70
Pope, Alexander, 83
Port Egmont, 65–6, 68–70, 73–4, 85, 89
Port Soledad, 67, 68, 70
Princess of Wales, 93

Quebec, 13, 93, 120–1

Ramillies, 36
Rhé Is., 5
Richelieu, Armand-Jean du Plessis, Cardinal, 75
Rochford, William Henry Zuylestein, Earl of, 74
Rockingham, Charles Watson-Wentworth, Marquis of, 87
Rome, 58, 114

St. Lucia (Martinique), 28
St. Maloes, 62
Sawbridge, John, 83
Selden, John, 45
Strong, John, 62
Stukely, Thomas, 108
Surrey, 89

Ticonderoga, *v.* Forts
Toulon, 36, 37
Townsend, James, 83
Truro, 125, 127
Tucker, Josiah (Dean of Gloucester), 116, 130
Tyler, Wat, 58

Utrecht, Peace of, 13

Venables, Robert, 7
Versailles, 32

Wales, 118
Wall, Richard, 64
Weert, Sebald de, 62
Westphalia, Treaty of, 74
Weymouth, Thomas Thynne, Viscount, 70
Wilkes, John, 40, 43–4, 51–2, 53, 83, 89, 92, 132
William III, 58, 62, 94
Woolwich, 69

Yorkshire, 55, 89

II. *Johnson's Works cited in the Introduction*

A Compleat Vindication of the Licensers of the Stage, x
Election addresses for Henry Thrale, xiv
The False Alarm, xiv–xvii
The Idler (in *Universal Chronicle*), xiii

Index

Index to *GM*, xi
Introduction to *Proceedings of the Committee for cloathing French Prisoners of War*, xiv
'Letter to Mr. Urban' (*GM*, 1739), ix
Literary Magazine: *An Appeal to the People concerning Admiral Byng*, etc., xiii
    An Introduction to the Political State of Great-Britain, xi–xii
    Memoirs of the King of Prussia, xiii
    Observations on a letter from 'Gallo-Anglus', xiii
    Observations on His Britannic Majesty's Treaties with Her Imperial Majesty of all the Russia's and the Landgrave of Hesse-Cassel, xii
    Observations on the Present State of Affairs, xii–xiii
    Reviews of Thomas Blackwell's *Memoirs of the Court of Augustus*, and Lewis Evans' *Essays on the Middle British Colonies in America*, xiv
    The Militia Bill, with remarks, xiii
London, ix
Marmor Norfolciense, ix
Observations (in *Universal Chronicle*), xiii
Parliamentary Debates, x
The Patriot, xvii–xviii
The Plays of William Shakespeare, xiv
Political Tracts, xxi
Preface to *The Preceptor*, xi
Review of William Tytler's *An Historical and Critical Enquiry into the Evidence against Mary Queen of Scots*, xiv
Taxation No Tyranny, xviii–xxi
Thoughts on the Late Transactions respecting Falkland's Islands, xvii

11-5-68
ONBK